The Undergraduate's Companion to Children's Writers and Their Web Sites

**Recent titles in the
Undergraduate Companion Series**

The Undergraduate's Companion to American Writers and Their Web Sites
James K. Bracken and Larry G. Hinman

The Undergraduate's Companion to Women Writers and Their Web Sites
Katharine A. Dean, Miriam Conteh-Morgan, and James K. Bracken

The Undergraduate's Companion to English Renaissance Writers and Their Web Sites
Steven Kenneth Galbraith

The Undergraduate's Companion to Women Poets of the World and Their Web Sites
Katharine A. Dean

The Undergraduate's Companion to Arab Writers and Their Web Sites
Dona S. Straley

The Undergraduate's Companion to Children's Writers and Their Web Sites

Jen Stevens

Undergraduate Companion Series

James K. Bracken, Series Editor

A Member of the Greenwood Publishing Group

Westport, Connecticut   London

Library of Congress Cataloging-in-Publication Data

Stevens, Jen, 1970–
  The undergraduate's companion to children's writers and their web sites / Jen Stevens.
    p. cm. — (Undergraduate companion series)
  Includes index.
  ISBN 1–59158–097–8 (pbk. : alk. paper)
    1. Children's literature, American—Bio-bibliography—Handbooks, manuals, etc. 2.
  Children—Books and reading—English-speaking countries—Handbooks, manuals, etc. 3.
  Children's literature, English—Bio-bibliography—Handbooks, manuals, etc. 4. American
  literature—20th century—Bio-bibliography—Handbooks, manuals, etc. 5. English
  literature—20th century—Bio-bibliography—Handbooks, manuals, etc. 6. Authors,
  American—Biography—Handbooks, manuals, etc. 7. Authors,
  English—Biography—Handbooks, manuals, etc. 8. Web sites—Handbooks, manuals, etc. I.
  Title. II. Series.
  PS490.S73   2004
  810.9'9282'0904—dc22   2004048639

British Library Cataloguing in Publication Data is available.

Library of Congress Catalog Card Number: 2004048639
ISBN: 1–59158–097–8

First published in 2004

Libraries Unlimited, 88 Post Road West, Westport, CT 06881
A Member of the Greenwood Publishing Group, Inc.
www.lu.com

Printed in the United States of America

The paper used in this book complies with the
Permanent Paper Standard issued by the National
Information Standards Organization (Z39.48–1984).

10 9 8 7 6 5 4 3 2 1

Contents

Acknowledgments vii

Introduction ix

Alphabetical List of Writers xiii

Frequently Cited Web Sites 1
Frequently Cited References 7
Web Sites and References for Authors 11

Index of Authors 151

Acknowledgments

Many thanks to all of my colleagues at Washington State University Libraries for their advice and support, especially Lorena O'English and Scott Walter. I'd also like to thank Jim Bracken for his guidance and encouragement during the course of this project.

Introduction

This book is part of the Undergraduate Companion series published by Libraries Unlimited. As with other books in the series, it includes both print and free online sources for research on authors. This volume focuses on American and British writers for children and young adults.

This book is directed toward undergraduate students who are taking courses in children's and young adult literature, which are often offered by English departments. Children's and young adult literature is also taught in education departments, and is often a requirement for students seeking primary or secondary teaching endorsements. Some colleges and universities offer these courses through both departments. For instance, at Washington State University, Young Adult Literature is an English course, while Children's Literature is a College of Education course.

Although this book is addressed to students in education classes, lesson plan web sites are not included. However, there are several excellent web portal sites for lesson plans, including The Gateway to Educational Materials (http://www.thegateway.org/). Nor have book reviews been included. Rather, the volume focuses on sites that offer biographical, critical, or historical information about authors that will be helpful to undergraduate students in a variety of contexts.

The Internet provides an array of different resources, including book cover scans, audio files of author interviews, full texts of books that are not copyrighted, critical articles, and current book lists. In turn, print resources provide solid biographical and critical information that complements and often expands on Internet resources. Together, Internet and print resources provide a more complete and complex portrait of an author. In the case of authors who are alive and currently publishing, online resources such as publisher web sites can give valuable insights into the ways an author's works are marketed to the reading public.

THE WRITERS

Entries for 185 British and American writers and writing teams for children and young adults are included. Although most are from the twentieth century, some children's writers who published prior to the twentieth century are also included, as well as some who, although they did not write primarily for children and young adults, were and are commonly read by those age groups. (Examples of the latter include Jane Austen and Jack London.) Among the criteria for selection were inclusion in children's and young adult literature textbooks and class syllabi; historical importance within the field of children's and young adult literature; and present currency in K–12 classrooms and among children and young adults. Rather than trying to select authors that fit all of these criteria (although a few, such as Laura Ingalls Wilder, did), I included representative authors for each.

Although 185 may seem like a large number, it is actually quite small when one considers the sheer number of British and American children's and young adult authors who have written books. Thus, many important children's and young adult writers had to be omitted because of space limitations. Others were not included because there was too little information available about them on the web when the research for this book was done. I have included both picture book and chapter book writers, but no illustrators unless they also wrote books.

WEB SITES

I selected web sites based on a number of criteria, including accuracy, fullness of information, and how current they were. My goal was to select sites with information that was as useful and timely as possible. Most sites selected include biographical information and lists of works, but sites providing critical pieces on particular works or aspects of a writer's career are also noted. Some sites have audio files, while others include full texts of all or part of an author's canon (these texts are mainly limited to works that are not copyrighted and thus in the public domain). Many of the web sites included are affiliated with a larger institution, but some excellent sites that are maintained by enthusiasts are also included. The selected web sites are directed to a variety of different audiences, including children, teachers, and scholars. Although the basic facts noted will be the same, the presentation of these facts may vary greatly. Like print sources, web sites can be wonderful places to find other sources, both print and online (one good source deserves another!). Although many web sites included in this book are annotated with a brief description of their contents, more complete annotations are provided in the "Frequently Cited Web Sites" chapter.

Web site URLs (addresses) often change over time. If you should come across an URL that no longer works, try the following:

- First, try a different web browser. Some pages won't work with a particular browser.
- Next, try looking up the title of the web page on an Internet search engine such as Google (www.google.com). Google also saves site information (this is known as "caching"), so try the "cached" link if the current link doesn't work.
- If the page is from a publisher web site, try an internal search in the web site (publishers often rearrange their sites and URLs).
- Finally, try looking up the nonworking URL in the Internet Archive (www.archive.org), an online archive for both active and obsolete web sites.

The archive doesn't include every page that's ever been online, but it includes a large number of them.

The Companion series focuses on freely available Internet resources and web sites, therefore the subscription databases available through many academic and some public libraries are not included. In addition to the Internet resources noted in this volume, you might also consult subscription databases such as *MLA International Bibliography*, the *Literature Resource Center* (LRC), the *Annual Bibliography of English Language and Literature* (ABELL), and *Literature Online* (LION).

REFERENCE WORKS

As mentioned above, print sources, particularly reference works, provide a wealth of biographical and critical information about writers. Reference works include encyclopedias, dictionaries, concordances, and bibliographies. Key reference sources are included for each writer, and are also noted in the "Frequently Cited References" chapter. The latter includes full citations and annotations; references to these works in the main text have been abbreviated.

ORGANIZATION OF ENTRIES

The entries are arranged alphabetically by the author's last name. Within each entry, web sites are noted first (in alphabetical order), followed by selected print reference sources. Within the web site listings, the last date of the site update and/or the copyright, as well as the date I last accessed the site are noted.

All spellings of author names and birth dates are based on standard authorities, including *The Continuum Encyclopedia of Children's Literature* (New York: Continuum, 2001) and *The Cambridge Guide to Children's Books in English* (Cambridge, UK: Cambridge University Press, 2001), and the pen name the writer usually uses or used for is noted (e.g., Avi).

EVERYTHING I WISH STUDENTS KNEW ABOUT DOING RESEARCH ON THE INTERNET

Researching writers using the Internet is actually harder in some ways than researching them using reference books. Not only is the web less well organized than a reference book, but the information on the web can also be much less reliable. Following are some points to keep in mind when evaluating a web site.

- *Currency:* How current is the site? Look for an "updated" date on the site. A page that is several years old can still have valid information about an author, but you'll want to look at more recent sources for information about an author's current work if the author is still alive. This goes for print sources as well. Moreover, an older web site may offer links to other sites that are no longer valid.

- *Authority:* Who created the site? What credentials do they have? Are they affiliated with a publication or an institution? If an individual author is not listed, what authority does the organization and/or site as a whole appear to have? There are some excellent "amateur" web sites out there (and some are included), but you'll need to be extra careful that your information is correct. For instance, I had to omit one otherwise sound page because it listed an incorrect date of birth for the author. Don't rely on one source alone—use others to verify the facts presented.

- *Point of View:* A publisher web site and an author profile from an online magazine may present the same facts, but in very different ways. Publisher pages are aimed at selling books, while author profiles by a third party may be neutral or even critical of an author's work. Read numerous sources for a variety of viewpoints.

- *Audience:* Articles from online scholarly journals, such as *The ALAN Review* (http://scholar.lib.vt.edu/ejournals/ALAN/), are aimed at a very different audience than are articles from web sites addressing children and young adults, such as *Kidspace @ the Internet Public Library* (http://www.ipl.org/div/kidspace). Which ones will serve you best depends on the type of research you are doing.

Web sites can be very valuable sources of information for children's writers. Just make sure you are an informed researcher.

Alphabetical List of Writers

Ada, Alma Flor, 1938–

Adams, Richard, 1920–

Adler, David, 1947–

Aiken, Joan, 1924–2004

Alcott, Louisa May, 1832–1888

Aldrich, Thomas Bailey, 1836–1907

Alexander, Lloyd, 1924–

Alger, Horatio, Jr., 1832–1899

Aliki (Brandenberg), 1929–

Andersen, Hans Christian, 1805–1875

Armstrong, William H., 1914–1999

Austen, Jane, 1775–1817

Avi (Wortis), 1937–

Awdry, Wilbert Vere, 1911–1997

Babbitt, Natalie, 1932–

Bagnold, Enid, 1889–1981

Ballantyne, R. M., 1825–1894

Barrie, J. M., 1860–1937

Baum, L. Frank, 1856–1919

Bawden, Nina, 1925–

Bellairs, John, 1938–1991

Bemelmans, Ludwig, 1898–1962

Berenstain, Jan, 1923– , and Berenstain, Stan, 1923–

Block, Francesca Lia, 1962–

Blume, Judy, 1938–

Blyton, Enid, 1897–1968

Bond, Michael, 1926–

Bridgers, Sue Ellen, 1942–

Briggs, Raymond, 1934–

Brooks, Gwendolyn, 1917–2000

Brown, Marc, 1946–

Brown, Margaret Wise, 1910–1952

Bruchac, Joseph, 1942–

Bunting, Eve, 1928–

Burnett, Frances Hodgson, 1849–1924

Burton, Virginia Lee, 1909–1968

Byars, Betsy, 1928–

Cabot, Meg, 1967–

Carle, Eric, 1929–

Carroll, Lewis. *See* Dodgson, Charles Lutwidge

Child, Lydia Maria, 1802–1880

Christopher, John, 1922–

Ciardi, John, 1916–1986

Cisneros, Sandra, 1954–

Cleary, Beverly, 1916–

Clemens, Samuel Langhorne (Mark Twain), 1835–1910

Clifton, Lucille, 1936–

Coatsworth, Elizabeth, 1893–1986

Collodi, Carlo (Carlo Lorenzini), 1826–1890

Cooney, Barbara, 1917–2000

Cooney, Caroline, 1947–

Cooper, Susan, 1935–

Cormier, Robert, 1925–2000

Creech, Sharon, 1945–

Crutcher, Chris, 1946–

Cushman, Karen, 1941–

Dahl, Roald, 1916–1990

Danziger, Paula, 1944–2004

de Angeli, Marguerite, 1889–1987

de Brunhoff, Jean, 1899–1937, and de Brunhoff, Laurent, 1925–

Defoe, Daniel, 1660–1731

dePaola, Tomie, 1934–

Dickens, Charles, 1812–1870

Dodgson, Charles Lutwidge (Lewis Carroll), 1832–1898

Doyle, Arthur Conan, 1859–1930

du Bois, William Pène, 1916–1993

Duncan, Lois, 1934–

Engdahl, Sylvia, 1933–

Erdrich, Louise, 1954–

Farley, Walter, 1915–1989

Fitzhugh, Louise, 1928–1974

Fleischman, Sid, 1920–

Fox, Paula, 1923–

Frank, Anne, 1929–1945

Fritz, Jean, 1915–

Gág, Wanda, 1893–1946

Gaiman, Neil, 1960–

Geisel, Theodor Seuss (Dr. Seuss), 1904–1991

George, Jean Craighead, 1919–

Gipson, Fred, 1908–1973

Gorey, Edward, 1925–2000

Grahame, Kenneth, 1859–1932

Greenaway, Kate, 1846–1901

Greenfield, Eloise, 1929–

Grimes, Nikki, 1950–

Grimm, Jacob Ludwig Karl, 1785–1863, and Grimm, Wilhelm Karl, 1786–1859

Gruelle, Johnny, 1880–1938

Hamilton, Virginia, 1936–2002

Handler, Daniel (Lemony Snicket), 1970–

Harris, Joel Chandler (Uncle Remus), 1848–1908

Henkes, Kevin, 1960–

Hinton, S. E., 1950–

Hoban, Lillian, 1925–1998

Hoban, Russell, 1925–

Hughes, Ted, 1930–1998

Jacques, Brian, 1939–

Jarrell, Randall, 1914–1965

Johnson, Crockett, 1906–1975

Joyce, William, 1957–

Keats, Ezra Jack, 1916–1983

Kerr, M. E., 1927–

Kipling, Rudyard, 1865–1936

Konigsburg, E. L., 1930–

Lamb, Charles, 1775–1834, and Lamb, Mary Ann, 1764–1847

Lang, Andrew, 1844–1912

Lawson, Robert, 1892–1957

Lear, Edward, 1812–1888

Le Guin, Ursula K., 1929–

L'Engle, Madeleine, 1918–

Lenski, Lois, 1893–1974

Lester, Julius, 1939–

Levine, Gail, 1947–

Lewis, C. S., 1898–1963

Lindgren, Astrid, 1907–2002

Lobel, Arnold, 1933–1987

Lofting, Hugh, 1886–1947

London, Jack, 1876–1916

Lorenzini, Carlo. *See* Collodi, Carlo

Lowry, Lois, 1937–

Macaulay, David, 1946–

MacDonald, George, 1824–1905

McCaffrey, Anne, 1926–

McCloskey, Robert, 1914–2003

McKinley, Robin, 1952–

Milne, A. A., 1882–1956

Minarik, Else Holmelund, 1920–

Montgomery, L. M., 1874–1942

Mora, Pat, 1942–

Myers, Walter Dean, 1937–

Nash, F. Ogden, 1902–1971

Nesbit, Edith, 1858–1924

Norton, Andre, 1912–

Norton, Mary, 1903–1992

O'Brien, Robert C., 1918–1973

O'Dell, Scott, 1898–1989

Paterson, Katherine, 1932–

Paton Walsh, Jill (Gillian), 1937–

Peck, Richard, 1934–

Peck, Robert Newton, 1928–

Pinkwater, Daniel, 1941–

Poe, Edgar Allan, 1809–1849

Potter, Beatrix, 1866–1943

Pullman, Philip, 1946–

Ransome, Arthur, 1884–1967

Raschka, Chris, 1959–

Raskin, Ellen, 1928–1984

Rawlings, Marjorie Kinnan, 1896–1953

Rey, H. A., 1898–1977, and Rey, Margret, 1906–1996

Rossetti, Christina Georgina, 1830–1894

Rowling, J. K., 1965–

Saint-Exupéry, Antoine de, 1900–1944

Scarry, Richard, 1919–1994

Scieszka, Jon, 1954–

Sendak, Maurice, 1928–

Seredy, Kate, 1899–1975

Seuss, Dr. *See* Geisel, Theodor Seuss (Dr. Seuss)

Sewell, Anna, 1820–1878

Silverstein, Shel, 1932–1999

Singer, Isaac Bashevis, 1904–1991

Sleator, William, 1945–

Snicket, Lemony. *See* Handler, Daniel

Snyder, Zilpha Keatley, 1927–

Soto, Gary, 1952–

Speare, Elizabeth George, 1908–1994

Spinelli, Jerry, 1941–

Spyri, Johanna, 1827–1901

Steig, William, 1907–2003

Stevenson, Robert Louis, 1850–1894

Stine, R. L., 1943–

Stratemeyer, Edward L., 1862–1930

Taylor, Mildred D., 1943–

Thurber, James, 1894–1961

Tolkien, J.R.R., 1892–1973

Townsend, Sue, 1946–

Travers, P. L., 1899–1996

Twain, Mark. *See* Clemens, Samuel Langhorne

Uncle Remus. *See* Harris, Joel Chandler

Van Allsburg, Chris, 1949–

Verne, Jules, 1828–1905

Viorst, Judith, 1931–

Voigt, Cynthia, 1942–

Wells, Rosemary, 1943–

White, E. B., 1899–1985

White, T. H., 1906–1964

Wilder, Laura Ingalls, 1867–1957

Wolff, Ashley, 1956–

Wynne Jones, Diana, 1934–

Yep, Laurence, 1948–

Yolen, Jane, 1939–

Zindel, Paul, 1936–2003

Zolotow, Charlotte, 1915–

Frequently Cited Web Sites

ALAN Review. Last accessed 22 Dec. 2003. http://scholar.lib.vt.edu/ejournals/ALAN/.
The *ALAN Review*, a scholarly journal on young adult literature, is published by the Assembly on Literature for Adolescents of the National Council of Teachers of English. The *Review* features scholarly research articles on authors and their works, as well as news items about young adult literature. Several issues are freely available online from the *Review*'s web site.

"Audio Interviews." *BBC*. Last accessed 22 Dec. 2003. http://www.bbc.co.uk/bbc four/audiointerviews.
Part of the British Broadcasting Company (BBC) web site, "Audio Interviews" includes short audio files of BBC interviews with various public figures (including authors). Individual entries may also include brief biographical sketches and/or links to related sites.

"Authors and Illustrators." *Houghton Mifflin Education Place*. 2001. Last accessed 16 Dec. 2003. http://www.eduplace.com/kids/.
Part of the larger Houghton Mifflin publisher web site, this site offers short biographical sketches of various Houghton Mifflin children's and young adult authors and illustrators. These sketches address teachers and students but contain useful information for researchers as well. Most of the sketches include a picture of the author or illustrator, and some include interviews with and/or autobiographical statements from the author or illustrator.

"BBC Books." *BBC*. Last accessed 22 Dec. 2003. http://www.bbc.co.uk/arts/books/.
Part of the British Broadcasting Company (BBC) web site, "BBC Books" includes biographical sketches of authors. Individual entries may also include lists of selected works and/or links to related sites.

BookPage. 2003. Last accessed 22 Dec. 2003. http://www.bookpage.com.
BookPage is a newsletter distributed by many bookstores and libraries. Its web site includes brief biographical profiles of and interviews with authors.

BookSense.com. 2003. Last accessed 17 Dec. 2003. http://www.booksense.com.
Sponsored by the American Booksellers Association, BookSense.com is a

collective web site for independent booksellers across the country. The site includes interviews with authors, many of which include biographical information as well as information about their books.

The Bulletin of the Center for Children's Books. Last accessed 22 Dec. 2003. http://www.alexia.lis.uiuc.edu/puboff/bccb/.

Published by the Center for Children's Books, the *Bulletin* has selected archival articles about authors and their works posted freely on its web sites (other articles are available to subscribers only).

"Cooperative Children's Book Center." *School of Education, University of Wisconsin-Madison.* Last accessed 23 Dec. 2003. http://www.education .wisc.edu/ccbc/.

The Cooperative Children's Book Center web site includes numerous resources on children's and young adult authors, including online videos of presentations and lectures given by authors.

CORAL (Caribbean Online Resource and Archive). 2002. Last accessed 22 Dec. 2003. http://www.caribbeanedu.com/coral/default.asp.

Designed to help teachers and students in the Caribbean, *CORAL*'s site is sponsored by ILLUMINAT Education Solutions, an educational technology company in the Caribbean. *CORAL* offers a variety of online information resources, including over 250 biographical sketches of authors in its "Biography" section, with special emphasis on Caribbean authors.

The de Grummond Children's Literature Collection. 2003. Last accessed 17 Dec. 2003. http://www.lib.usm.edu/~degrum/.

Part of the University of Southern Mississippi Libraries, the *de Grummond Children's Collection* is a leading special collection for children's and young adult literature. The collection includes both books and archival materials such as letters and manuscripts. The collection provides several online exhibits about young adult and children's authors. Moreover, online research aids include biographical information, discussion of the author's work, and references to secondary materials that can provide additional information about the author. Secondary materials include books, articles, and web pages written *about* a given author work.

Educational Paperback Association. Last accessed 17 Dec. 2003. http://www.edu paperback.org.

The *Educational Paperback Association* is a group of publishers and book distributors that works with schools and libraries. The association includes biographical sketches for over 100 children's and young adult authors on its web site. These sketches often include references to other articles or web sites about the author.

Fantastic Fiction. 2003. Last accessed 17 Dec. 2003. http://www.fantasticfiction .co.uk/.

Includes bibliographies for over 4,000 British and American authors whose books could be considered part of the fantasy, science fiction, mystery, thriller, and horror genres. Some entries include portraits and biographical statements. Bibliographies include the titles and images of book jackets of selected primary works (books and stories written by the author). Some also include secondary works (books and articles written about the author and/or the author's works).

HarperChildrens.com. Last accessed 22 Dec. 2003. http://www.harperchildrens
.com/index.asp.

Publisher web site. Includes biographical sketches about and interviews with various children's and young adult authors. The material is directed toward parents, teachers, and children, but contains much valuable information for researchers.

HarperCollins.com. 2003. Last accessed 29 Dec. 2003. http://www.harpercollins
.com/hc/home.asp.

Publisher web site. Includes biographical sketches about various children's and young adult authors. The material is directed toward the book-buying public, as well as parents, children, and teachers. Much of it is also valuable for researchers.

The Horn Book. 2003. Last accessed 22 Dec. 2003. http://www.hbook.com.

The *Horn Book* is one of the oldest and most respected children's literature review journals. Its site includes a "Virtual History" section that contains audio files of interviews with a number of children's and young adult authors.

Hurst, Carol Otis, and Rebecca Otis. *Carol Hurst's Children's Literature Web Site.* 1999. Last accessed 22 Dec. 2003. http://www.carolhurst.com/.

Directed toward teachers and librarians, this site features numerous resources on children's literature, including author profiles and curriculum plans.

Kidsreads.com. 2003. Last accessed 17 Dec. 2003. http://www.kidsreads.com.

Directed toward children and part of the Book Report Network, Kidsreads
.com is a site about children's books and authors. The author profiles, however, include information about authors and their books that is also useful for researchers. Some entries include a portrait of the author and/or list of selected works by the author.

Literary Traveler: Explore Your Imagination. Ed. Francis McGovern. 2003. Last accessed 17 Dec. 2003. http://www.literarytraveler.com.

This electronic magazine includes sketches about authors and the landscapes and locations they lived in or used in their work with the aim of promoting a fuller understanding of the contexts for the authors and their work. Past articles are archived.

Liukkonen, Petri. "Author's Calendar." *Pegasus.* Ed. Ari Pesonen. 2000. Last accessed 17 Dec. 2003. http://www.kirjasto.sci.fi/calendar.htm.

Part of the *Pegasus* literature site, the "Author's Calendar" provides short, well-written biographical sketches of both current and classic authors. Lists of works by and about the authors are also provided.

The Looking Glass: New Perspectives on Children's Books. 2003. Last accessed 22 Dec. 2003. http://www.the-looking-glass.net.

The *Looking Glass* is an online journal for children's and young adult literature that includes both news and scholarly articles about authors and their works.

Modern American Poetry. Ed. Cary Nelson. 2002. Last accessed 22 Dec. 2003.
http://www.english.uiuc.edu/maps/index.htm.
   Sponsored by the University of Illinois at Urbana-Champaign Department
of English, this site includes profiles of over 150 modern American poets. Individual entries may include critical articles on the poet in question, online images
of original manuscripts, and links to related sites. The site has a strong research
focus and is intended for students and scholars.

Ortakales, Denise. *Women Children's Illustrators.* Last accessed 11 Dec. 2003.
http://www.ortakales.com/illustrators/.
   Ortakales' site includes biographical articles about a number of women
children's authors who also illustrated their books or those of other authors. Individual entries may include illustrator portraits or illustrations.

Penguin Group USA. 22 Dec. 2003. Last accessed 22 Dec. 2003. http://www
.penguinputnam.com.
   Publisher web site. Includes biographical sketches of children's and young
adult authors, as well as special pages for selected series and books. The sketches
are intended to promote the authors and are directed towards teachers and parents,
but give much valuable information.

"Poetry Exhibits." *The Academy of American Poets.* 2003. Last accessed 22 Dec.
2003. http://www.poets.org/poets/poets.cfm.
   Includes biographical profiles of various poets. Individual entries may include links to related web sites.

Project Gutenberg. 4 May 2003. Last accessed 22 Dec. 2003. http://www
.gutenberg.net/index.shtml.
   Project Gutenberg is one the largest digital collections of uncopyrighted
works. The site includes a search interface for locating text by author or title.

"Reading Zone." *Kidspace @ The Internet Public Library.* 1996. Last accessed
22 Dec. 2003. http://www.ipl.org/div/kidspace/.
   Sponsored by the University of Michigan School of Information, this web
site features information for children, teachers, and parents on a variety of topics.
The "Reading Zone" includes information about books and authors, as well as
links to online texts and related sites. Although the author interviews are directed
toward children, teachers, and parents, they include valuable biographical information for researchers.

Reuben, Paul P. *PAL: Perspectives in American Literature—A Research and Reference Guide—An Ongoing Project.* 19 Nov. 2003. Last accessed 17 Dec.
2003. http://www.csustan.edu/english/reuben/home.htm.
   Maintained by Paul P. Reuben, an English professor at California State University Stanislaus, this site presents lists of primary works (works written by the
author) and online and print resources for over 360 American authors, both past
and present.

Scholastic. 2003. Last accessed 17 Dec. 2003. http://www.scholastic.com/.
   Scholastic is one of the larger publishers for children's and young adult
books in the United States. Their site includes biographical profiles for many of

their authors. The profiles are designed to promote the author as well as to provide basic biographical information.

Scottish Authors. 1 July 2000. 23 Apr. 2001. Last accessed 22 Dec. 2003. http://www.slainte.org.uk/Scotauth/scauhome.htm.
  Sponsored by the Scottish Library Association, this web site is an online version of the print publication *Discovering Scottish Writers.* Author profiles include biographical information and discussion of selected works.

Teenreads.com. 2003. Last accessed 22 Dec. 2003. http://www.teenreads.com.
  Part of the Book Report Network, Teenreads.com is a site about young adult books and authors directed toward teens. However, the author profiles include information that is also useful for researchers. Some entries include a portrait or list of selected works by the author.

University of Texas Harry Ransome Humanities Research Center. Last accessed 22 Dec. 2003. http://www.hrc.utexas.edu/.
  The *Harry Ransome Humanities Research Center* web site includes research guides for many of the authors included in its archival collections. These research guides include biographical sketches.

Vandergrift, Kay. *Vandergrift's Children's Literature Page.* Last accessed 22 Dec. 2003. http://www.scils.rutgers.edu/~kvander.
  Created and maintained by Kay Vandergrift, a professor at Rutger University's School of Communication, Information, and Library Studies, this site features biographical profiles of children's and young adult authors.

The Victorian Web. Ed. George P. Landow. Last accessed 22 Dec. 2003. http://www .victorianweb.org.
  The Victorian Web is a project founded and maintained by George P. Landow, a professor of English at Brown University. It is currently funded by the National University of Singapore and includes biographical information on nineteenth century authors, discussion of their major works, and links to related web sites. Intended for students and scholars, the site has a strong research focus.

Voices from the Gaps: Women Writers of Color. 2003. Last accessed 22 Dec. 2003. http://voices.cla.umn.edu/newsite/.
  Sponsored by the University of Minnesota's English Department, *Voices from the Gap* features signed biographical sketches of North American women writers of color. Individual entries may include references to other works discussing the author, as well as links to related web sites. The site is intended for students and scholars and has a strong research focus.

Wilde, Susie. *Once upon a Lap.* Last accessed 23. Dec. 2003. http://wildes.home .mindspring.com/OUAL/front.html.
  Wilde is a "writer, reviewer, teacher, and workshop presenter" who has posted several of her previously published children's and young adult book reviews and author interviews on her own web site. Her site also includes sound files from radio broadcasts, book reviews, essays, and links to related online resources.

Wired for Books. Last accessed 22 Dec. 2003. http://wiredforbooks.org.

A production of the Ohio University Telecommunications Center, *Wired for Books* is a radio program featuring interviews with authors. The *Wired for Books* web site includes audio files of those interviews.

Frequently Cited References

Authors and Artists for Young People. Detroit, MI: Gale, 1989– .
    Entries include biographical information about authors and descriptions of the books, stories, and poems they wrote. May include references for further study. Some overlap with the "Something About the Author" series.

Battestin, Martin C., ed. *British Novelists, 1660–1800. Part 1: A–L*. (*Dictionary of Literary Biography* 39). Detroit, MI: Gale, 1985.
    Entries include discussion of authors' lives and the novels they wrote. Includes authors whose novels are often read by children and young adults. May include references for further study.

Cech, John, ed. *American Writers for Children, 1900–1960* (*Dictionary of Literary Biography* 22). Detroit, MI: Gale, 1983.
    Entries include discussion of authors' lives and of the novels, poems, and stories they wrote for children. May include references for further study.

Children's Literature Review. Detroit, MI: Gale, 1976– .
    Biographical entries and discussions of the novels, poems, and stories written by a given author. Includes excepts from book review and critical essays.

Contemporary Literary Criticism. Detroit, MI: Gale, 1973– .
    Biographical entries that include information about the novels, stories, and poems a given author wrote. May include references for further study.

Cullinan, Bernice E., and Diane G. Person, eds. *The Continuum Encyclopedia of Children's Literature*. New York: Continuum, 2001.
    Short biographical entries, including discussion of major works. May include references for further study.

Estes, Glenn E., ed. *American Writers for Children Before 1900* (*Dictionary of Literary Biography* 42). Detroit, MI: Gale, 1985.
    Entries include discussion of authors' lives and descriptions of the novels, poems, and stories they wrote for children. May include references for further study.

————, ed. *American Writers for Children Since 1960: Fiction* (*Dictionary of Literary Biography* 52). Detroit, MI: Gale, 1986.

Entries include discussion of authors' lives and the novels and stories they wrote for children. May include references for further study.

————, ed. *American Writers for Children Since 1960: Poets, Illustrators, and Nonfiction Authors* (*Dictionary of Literary Biography* 61). Detroit, MI: Gale, 1987.
Entries include discussion of the authors' lives and the poetry and nonfiction they wrote for children. Includes entries on illustrators, many of whom wrote as well as illustrated books. May include references for further study.

Harris-Fain, Darren, ed. *British Fantasy and Science-Fiction Writers, 1918–1960* (*Dictionary of Literary Biography* 255). Detroit, MI: Gale, 2002.
Biographical entries on fantasy and science-fiction writers, many of whose works are read by children and young adults. May include references for further study.

————, ed. *British Fantasy and Science-Fiction Writers Since 1960* (*Dictionary of Literary Biography* 261). Detroit, MI: Gale, 2002.
Biographical entries on fantasy and science-fiction writers, many of whose works are read by children and young adults. May include references for further study.

Hendrickson, Linnea. *Children's Literature: A Guide to the Criticism.* Boston: G. K. Hall, 1987.
Lists articles and books about authors and their works.

Hettinga, Donald R., and Gary D. Schmidt, eds. *British Children's Writers, 1914–1960* (*Dictionary of Literary Biography* 160). Detroit, MI: Gale, 1996.
Entries include discussion of the authors' lives and the novels, stories, and poems they wrote for children. May include references for further study.

Hunt, Caroline C., ed. *British Children's Writers Since 1960* (*Dictionary of Literary Biography* 161). Detroit, MI: Gale, 1996.
Entries include discussion of the authors' lives and the novels, stories, and poems they wrote for children. May include references for further study.

————, ed. *Four Writers for Children, 1868–1918: An Illustrated Chronicle* (*Dictionary of Literary Biography Documentary Series* 14). Detroit, MI: Gale, 1996.
Lengthy biographical essays; includes discussion of the poems, novels, and stories written by a given author. Includes list of works by and about authors.

Khorana, Meena, ed. *British Children's Writers, 1800–1880* (*Dictionary of Literary Biography* 163). Detroit, MI: Gale, 1996.
Entries include discussion of the writers' lives and the novels, stories, and poems they wrote for children. May include references for further study.

Lynn, Ruth Nadelman. *Fantasy Literature for Children and Young Adults.* 4th ed. New York: R. R. Bowker, 1995.
Lists articles and books about authors and their works.

Nineteenth-Century Literature Criticism. Detroit, MI: Gale, 1981– .
Biographical entries with extensive information about a given writer's stories, poems, or novels and how they were received by readers and critics. May include references for further study.

Rahn, Suzanne. *Children's Literature: An Annotated Bibliography of the History and Criticism*. New York: Garland, 1981.
Lists articles and books about authors and their works. Entries are annotated with brief descriptions of their contents.

Silvey, Anita, ed. *Children's Books and Their Creators*. Boston: Houghton Mifflin, 1995.
Brief biographical entries, including discussion of major works. May include references for further study.

———, ed. *The Essential Guide to Children's Books and Their Creators*. Boston: Houghton Mifflin, 2003.
Brief biographical entries, including discussion of major works. May include references for further study.

Something About the Author. Detroit, MI: Gale, 1971– .
Biographical entries, many of which include pictures of the author. May include a discussion of the author's poems, novels, or stories. May include references for further study. Some overlap with the "Authors and Artists for Young People" series.

Twentieth-Century Literature Criticism. Detroit, MI: Gale, 1978– .
Biographical entries, including discussion of major works. May include references for further study.

Zaidman, Laura M., ed. *British Children's Writers, 1880–1914* (*Dictionary of Literary Biography* 141). Detroit, MI: Gale, 1994.
Entries include discussion of writers' lives and the novels, poems, and stories they wrote for children. May include references for further study.

Web Sites and References for Authors

ALMA FLOR ADA, 1938–

Web Sites

Alma Flor Ada. 6 Nov. 2003. http://www.almaada.com/.
  Author web site. Includes primary bibliography, portrait, autobiographical sketch.

"Meet the Author: Alma Flor Ada." *Houghton Mifflin Education Place*. 6 Nov. 2003. http://www.eduplace.com/kids/hmr/mtai/ada.html.
  From publisher web site. Includes brief biographical sketch, portrait, list of books available from publisher.

Biographies and Criticism

"Ada, Alma Flor." *Something About the Author* 84: 1–7.
  Biographical sketch.

Ada, Alma Flor. *Under the Royal Palms: A Childhood in Cuba*. New York: Atheneum Books for Young Readers, 1998.
  Autobiography.

"Alma Flor Ada." *Children's Literature Review* 62: 1–14.
  Biographical sketch, excerpts from reviews.

Cullinan, Bernice E. "Ada, Alma Flor." Cullinan and Person, *The Continuum Encyclopedia of Children's Literature*. 4–5.
  Short biographical entry.

RICHARD ADAMS, 1920–

Web Sites

Bridgman, Joan. "Richard Adams at Eighty." *Contemporary Review*. Aug. 2000. Find Articles. Last accessed 7 Nov. 2003. http://www.findarticles.com/ m2242/1615_277/64752236/p1/article.jhtml.
Biographic piece on Richard Adams. Includes some discussion of his literary career.

"Richard Adams." *CORAL (Caribbean Online Resource and Archive)*. 2002. Last accessed 22 Dec. 2003. http://www.caribbeanedu.com/coral/refcen/ Biography/readbio.asp?id=4.
Biographical sketch.

"Richard Adams." *Fantastic Fiction*. 7 Nov. 2003. http://www.fantasticfiction.co .uk/authors/Richard_Adams.htm.
Lists Adams's works.

Biographies and Criticism

Adams, Richard. *The Day Gone By: An Autobiography*. London: Hutchinson, 1990.
Autobiography.

"Adams, Richard." *Something About the Author* 69: 1–3.
Biographical essay about Adams and his major works.

Ash, Gwynne Ellen. "Adams, Richard (George)." Cullinan and Person, *The Continuum Encyclopedia of Children's Literature*. 5–6.

Hile, Janet L. "Richard Adams." *Authors and Artists for Young Adults* 16: 1–12.
Biographical essay about Adams and his major works.

"Richard George Adams." *Children's Literature Review* 20: 10–32.
Biographical sketch with portrait; excerpts from reviews and literary criticism.

Sieruta, Peter D. "Adams, Richard." Silvey, *Children's Books and Their Creators*. 1–2.
Short biographical sketch.

Bibliographies

"Adams, Richard." Lynn, *Fantasy Literature for Children and Young Adults*. 598–600.
Lists books and articles about Adams.

Hendrickson, Linda. "Adams, Richard." *Children's Literature: A Guide to the Criticism*. 1–2.
Lists books and articles about Adams and his works.

DAVID ADLER, 1947–

Web Sites

David. A. Adler. Last accessed 11 Nov. 2003. http://www.davidaadler.com/.
Author's home page. Includes biographical information, list of major works.

"Meet Celebrity Author David Adler." *Scott Foresman.* Last accessed 11 Nov.
2003. http://www.scottforesman.com/families/authors/adler.html.
Brief biographical sketch, discussion of selected works.

"Meet the Author: David A. Adler." *Houghton Mifflin Education Place.* 2001. Last
accessed 11 Nov. 2003. http://www.eduplace.com/kids/hmr/mtai/adler.html.
From publisher web site. Includes brief biographical sketch, portrait, list of
books available from publisher.

Biographies and Criticism

Broughton, Mary Ariail. "Adler, David." Cullinan and Person, *The Continuum
Encyclopedia of Children's Literature.* 6–8.
Biographical sketch.

Jones, J. Sydney. "Adler, David A." *Something About the Author* 106: 1–9.
Biographical sketch and discussion of major works.

JOAN AIKEN, 1924–2004

Web Sites

Grant, Gavin J. "Very Interesting People: Joan Aiken." *Booksense.com.* Last accessed
11 Nov. 2003. http://www.booksense.com/people/archive/aikenjoan.jsp.
Interview with Aiken.

"Joan Aiken Bibliography." *Fantastic Fiction.* Last accessed 11 Nov. 2003.
http://www.fantasticfiction.co.uk/authors/Joan_Aiken.htm.
Lists Aiken's major works.

"Joan Aiken Papers." *de Grummond Collection.* June 2001. Last accessed 11 Nov.
2003. http://www.lib.usm.edu/%7Edegrum/html/research/findaids/aiken.htm.
Description of Joan Aiken archival papers in the de Grummond Collection.
Includes biographical sketch, discussion of major works.

"Joan Aiken: Wolves and Alternate Worlds." *Locus Online.* May 1998. Last accessed
11 Nov. 2003. http://www.locusmag.com/1998/Issues/05/Aiken.html.
Short biographical sketch, including several paragraphs by Aiken about her
works.

Biographies and Criticism

Clere, Sarah V. "Joan Aiken." Hunt, *British Children's Writers Since 1960
(Dictionary of Literary Biography* 161): 3–11.
Discussion of literary career and influence.

"Joan Aiken." *Children's Literature Review* 90: 1–33.
Discussion of critical reception of Aiken's works. Includes excerpts from reviews, literary criticism.

Kantar, Andrew. "Aiken, Joan (Delano)." Cullinan and Person, *The Continuum Encyclopedia of Children's Literature*. 16–17.
Short biographical sketch.

Rampson, Nancy. "Joan Aiken." *Authors and Artists for Young People* 25: 1–12.
Biographical sketch, discussion of literary career.

Slone, Cooki Holtze, "Aiken, Joan." Silvey, *Children's Books and Their Creators*. 9–10.
Short biographical sketch.

Bibliographies

"Aiken, Joan." Hendrickson, *Children's Literature: A Guide to the Criticism*. 4–5.
Lists books and articles about Aiken and her works.

"Joan Aiken." Rahn, *Children's Literature: An Annotated Bibliography of the History and Criticism*. 141–42.
Lists books and articles about Aiken and her works.

LOUISA MAY ALCOTT, 1832–1888

Web Sites

"*Little Women.*" *University of Virginia*. 1 Sept. 1995. Last accessed 11 Nov. 2003. http://xroads.virginia.edu/~HYPER/ALCOTT/LWHP.html.
Hypermedia presentation of *Little Women*. Includes biographical sketch of Alcott, online text of *Little Women*, primary and secondary bibliographies.

Liukkonen, Petri. "L(ouisa) M(ay) Alcott." *Author's Calendar*. Ed. Ari Pesonen. 2000. Last accessed 11 Nov. 2003. http://www.kirjasto.sci.fi/lmalcott.htm.
Biographical sketch and discussion of Alcott's major works.

Orchard House—Home of the Alcotts. 27 Oct. 2003. Last accessed 11 Nov. 2003. http://www.louisamayalcott.org/.
Web site for Orchard House, a museum and historical landmark. Site includes biographical information about Alcott and her family.

Project Gutenberg. 25 Dec. 2003. Last accessed 27 Dec. 2003. http://www.gutenberg.net/index.shtml.
Includes online texts for several of Alcott's novels, including *Little Women* and *Eight Cousins* (use the "Find an Ebook" link to find texts by Alcott).

Reuben, Paul P. "Chapter 5: Late Nineteenth Century—Louisa May Alcott (1832–1888)." *PAL: Perspectives in American Literature—A Research and*

Reference Guide. 3 Jan. 2003. Last accessed 11 Nov. 2003. http://www
.csustan.edu/english/reuben/pal/chap5/lalcott.html.
Includes primary and secondary bibliographies, portrait, links to related sites.

Biographies and Criticism

"Alcott, Louisa May." *Something About the Author* 100: 1–5.
Biographical sketch and discussion of her major works.

Holtze, Sally Holmes. "Alcott, Louisa May." Silvey, *Children's Books and Their
Creators*. 10–12.
Biographical sketch.

Keyser, Elizabeth Lennox. *Whispers in the Dark: The Fiction of Louisa May
Alcott*. Knoxville: University of Tennessee Press, 1993.
Book-length critical discussion of Alcott's works.

"Louisa May Alcott." *Children's Literature Review* 38: 1–63.
Discussion of Alcott's literary career and critical reception, including excerpts from reviews and literary criticism.

"Louisa May Alcott." Hunt, *Four Writers for Children, 1868–1918: An Illustrated
Chronicle* (*Dictionary of Literary Biography Documentary Series* 14): 3–94.
Lengthy discussion of literary career and influence.

MacDonald, Ruth K. "Louisa May Alcott." Estes, *American Writers for Children
Before 1900* (*Dictionary of Literary Biography* 42): 18–36.
Discussion of Alcott's life and literary career.

Dictionaries, Encyclopedias, and Handbooks

Eiselein, Gregory, and Anne K. Phillips, eds. *Louisa May Alcott Encyclopedia*.
Westport, CT: Greenwood, 2001.
Includes entries on various aspects of Alcott's life and literary career.

Bibliographies

"Alcott, Louisa May." Hendrickson, *Children's Literature: A Guide to the Criticism*. 5–10.
Lists articles and books about Alcott and her works.

"Louisa May Alcott." Rahn, *Children's Literature: An Annotated Bibliography of
the History and Criticism*. 143–48.
Lists articles and books about Alcott and her works.

THOMAS BAILEY ALDRICH, 1836–1907

Web Sites

Project Gutenberg. 25 Dec. 2003. Last accessed 27 Dec. 2003. http://www
.gutenberg.net/index.shtml.

Includes uncopyrighted online texts for several of Aldrich's works, including *The Story of a Bad Boy* (use the "Find an Ebook" link to find texts by Aldrich).

Robinson, J. Dennis. "Portsmouth's Bad Boy: Thomas Bailey Aldrich." *Seacoast NH.com*. 1998. Last accessed 11 Nov. 2003. http://www.seacoastnh.com/aldrich/bio.html#page1.
Includes portraits, biographical sketch, and links to related sites.

"The Thomas Bailey Aldrich Memorial." *Strawbery Banke*. Last accessed 11 Nov. 2003. http://www.strawberybanke.org/museum/aldrich/aldrich.html.
Biographical information, portraits.

Biographies and Criticism

"Aldrich, Thomas (Bailey)." *Something About the Author* 114: 1–3.
Biographical sketch and discussion of major works.

Wolf, Virginia L. "Thomas Bailey Aldrich." Estes, *American Writers for Children Before 1900* (*Dictionary of Literary Biography* 42): 42–52.
Discussion of Aldrich's life and literary career.

Bibliographies

"Thomas Bailey Aldrich." Rahn, *Children's Literature: An Annotated Bibliography of the History and Criticism*. 148.
Lists books and articles about Aldrich and his works.

LLOYD ALEXANDER, 1924–

Web Sites

"Lloyd Alexander." *Kidsreads.com*. 2000. Last accessed 11 Nov. 2003. http://www.kidsreads.com/authors/au-alexander-lloyd.asp.
Biographical sketch of Alexander.

"Lloyd Alexander Bibliography." *Fantastic Fiction*. Last accessed 11 Nov. 2003. http://www.fantasticfiction.co.uk/authors/Lloyd_Alexander.htm.
Lists Alexander's major works.

"Lloyd Alexander's Biography." *Scholastic*. Last accessed 11 Nov. 2003. http://www2.scholastic.com/teachers/authorsandbooks/authorstudies/authorhome.jhtml?authorID=1&collateralID=5073&displayName=Biography.
From publisher web site. Includes links to a list of Alexander's books that are available from the publisher and an interview with Alexander.

The Prydain Guide: Wisdom for Your Poor, Tender Head. 10 Oct. 2002. Last accessed 11 Nov. 2003. http://www.enkwiri.com/prydain/.
Extensive web site devoted to Alexander's Prydain Chronicles. Includes information about characters, items, and places from the Chronicles. Also includes an extensive list of links to web sites pertaining to Alexander.

Biographies and Criticism

"Alexander, Lloyd (Chudley)." *Something About the Author* 135: 1–7.
   Discussion of Alexander's life and literary career.

Deifendeifer, Anne E. "Alexander, Lloyd." Silvey, *Children's Books and Their Creators.* 12–14.
   Short biographical sketches.

Ingram, Laura. "Lloyd Alexander." Estes, *American Writers for Children Since 1960: Fiction (Dictionary of Literary Biography* 52): 3–21.
   Extensive discussion of Alexander's literary career and impact.

"Lloyd Alexander." *Children's Literature Review* 48: 1–30.
   Biographical sketch, interview with Alexander, and excerpts from reviews and literary criticism about Alexander's works.

May, Jill. *Lloyd Alexander.* Boston: Twayne Publishers, 1991.
   Critical commentary on Alexander's works.

Bibliographies

"Alexander, Lloyd (Chudley)." Lynn, *Fantasy Literature for Children and Young Adults.* 603–7.
   Lists books and articles about Alexander and his works.

"Lloyd Alexander." Rahn, *Children's Literature: An Annotated Bibliography of the History and Criticism.* 10–11.
   Lists books and articles about Alexander and his works.

HORATIO ALGER, JR., 1832–1899

Web Sites

"Horatio Alger (1832–99)." *American Literature on the Web.* 28 Aug. 2000. Last accessed 11 Nov. 2003. http://www.nagasaki-gaigo.ac.jp/ishikawa/amlit/a/alger19re.htm.
   Extensive list of links to web sites about or pertaining to Alger and his works.

"The Horatio Alger Collection / Horatio Alger, Jr." *Rare Books & Special Collections, Northern Illinois University Libraries.* 12 March 2003. Last accessed 11 Nov. 2003. http://www.niulib.niu.edu/rbsc/2ha2.html.
   Biographical sketch. Includes links to related online collections.

Project Gutenberg. 25 Dec. 2003. Last accessed 27 Dec. 2003. http://www.gutenberg.net/index.shtml.
   Includes online texts for over twenty of Alger's works, including *Ragged Dick, or, Street Life in New York with the Boot-Blacks.* Use the "Find an Ebook" link to find texts by Alger.

Reuben, Paul P. "Chapter 5: Late Nineteenth Century—Horatio Alger (1832–1899)." *PAL: Perspectives in American Literature—A Research and*

Reference Guide. 21 July 2003. Last accessed 11 Nov. 2003. http://www
.csustan.edu/english/reuben/pal/chap5/alger.html.
Includes primary and secondary bibliographies, portrait, links to related
sites.

Biographies and Criticism

"Alger, Horatio, Jr." *Something About the Author* 16: 3–11.
Biographical sketch with time line.

Barclay, Donald A. "Alger, Horatio, Jr.," Silvey, *Children's Books and Their Creators.* 14–15.
Short biographical sketch.

"Horatio Alger, Jr." *Children's Literature Review* 87: 1–113.
Biographical sketch, discussion of literary career, excerpts from reviews
and commentary.

Karrenbrock, Marilyn H. "Horatio Alger, Jr." Estes, *American Writers for Children Before 1900* (*Dictionary of Literary Biography* 42): 52–73.
Extensive biographical sketch and discussion of Alger's literary career.

Bibliographies

"Horatio Alger, Jr." Rahn, *Children's Literature: An Annotated Bibliography of
the History and Criticism.* 148–54.
Lists books and articles about Alger and his works.

ALIKI (BRANDENBERG), 1929–

Web Sites

"Aliki." *Kaleidoscope 6.* 15 July 1996. Last accessed 11 Nov. 2003. http://
www.ucalgary.ca/~dkbrown/k6/aliki.html.
Biographical sketch with portrait.

"Aliki Brandenberg Papers." *de Grummond Collection.* 7 June 2001. Last
accessed 11 Nov. 2003. http://www.lib.usm.edu/~degrum/html/research/
findaids/brandenb.htm.
Description of Aliki's archival papers in the de Grummond Collection.
Includes biographical sketch, discussion of major works.

"Author Tracker: Aliki." *HarperCollins.* Last accessed 23 Dec. 2003. http://
www.harpercollins.com/catalog/author_xml.asp?AuthorId=11719.
Biographical sketch.

Biographies and Criticism

"Aliki." *Children's Literature Review* 71: 1–24.
Discussion of Aliki's literary career, impact. Includes excerpts from reviews.

Jones, Sydney J. "Brandenberg, Aliki." *Something About the Author* 113: 16–22.
Biographical sketch and discussion of major works.

Neuburg, Helen Green. "Aliki." Silvey, *Children's Books and Their Creators*. 15–16.
Short biographical sketch.

HANS CHRISTIAN ANDERSEN, 1805–1875

Web Sites

Hanford, Juliana. "Hans Christian Andersen." *Literary Traveler*. Last accessed
11 Nov. 2003. http://www.literarytraveler.com/hanschristianandersen/hans-christian-andersen.htm.
Biographical sketch.

The Hans Christian Andersen Center. 24 Sept. 2003. Last accessed 11 Nov. 2003.
http://www.andersen.sdu.dk/index_e.html.
Site includes biographical information, research resources, and information
on Andersen's work.

Har'El, Zvi. *Hans Christian Andersen Annotated Web-o-graphy*. 21 Nov. 2002.
Last accessed 11 Nov. 2003. http://hca.gilead.org.il/www.html.
Annotated page of links to various Andersen-related sites.

Liukkonen, Petri. "Hans Christian Andersen." *Author's Calendar*. Ed. Ari Pesonen.
2000. Last accessed 11 Nov. 2003. http://www.kirjasto.sci.fi/hcanders.htm.
Biographical sketch and discussion of Andersen's major works. Includes
primary and secondary bibliographies.

Project Gutenberg. 25 Dec. 2003. Last accessed 27 Dec. 2003. http://www
.gutenberg.net/index.shtml.
Includes online texts for several of Andersen's works, including *The Emperor's New Clothes* and *The True Story of My Life*. Use the "Find an Ebook" link
to find texts by Andersen.

Biographies and Criticism

"Andersen, Hans Christian." *Something About the Author* 100: 5–12.
Biographical sketch, extensive bibliography of his works and adaptations of
them.

Geraty, Sheila McMorrow. "Andersen, Hans Christian." Silvey, *Children's Books
and Their Creators*. 24–26.
Short biographical sketch.

"Hans Christian Andersen." *Children's Literature Review* 6: 17–47.
Biographical sketch with portrait; general commentary on Andersen's literary works, especially his collections of fairy tales.

Mathis, Janelle B. "Andersen, Hans Christian." Cullinan and Person, *The Continuum Encyclopedia of Children's Literature*. 33–35.
Biographical sketch.

Bibliographies

"Andersen, Hans Christian." Lynn, *Fantasy Literature for Children and Young Adults*. 607–11.
Lists books and articles about Andersen and his works.

"Hans Christian Andersen." Rahn, *Children's Literature: An Annotated Bibliography of the History and Criticism*. 154–60.
List of books and articles about Andersen and his works.

WILLIAM H. ARMSTRONG, 1914–1999

Web Sites

"Armstrong, William." *Educational Paperback Association*. Last accessed 11 Nov. 2003. http://www.edupaperback.org/showauth.cfm?authid=10.
Biographical sketch with list of major works.

"William Armstrong." *CORAL (Caribbean Online Resource and Archive)*. 2002. Last accessed 22 Dec. 2003. http://www.caribbeanedu.com/coral/refcen/Biography/readbio.asp?id=18.
Biographical sketch.

Biographies and Criticism

Amster, Mara Ilyse. "Armstrong, William." Silvey, *Children's Books and Their Creators*. 30–31.
Short biographical sketch.

"Armstrong, William H(oward)." *Children's Literature Review* 1: 22–25.
Excerpts from reviews of Armstrong's works.

Sukraw, Tracy J. "William H. Armstrong." *Authors and Artists for Young People* 18: 9–15.
Biographical sketch and discussion of major works.

JANE AUSTEN, 1775–1817

Web Sites

Liukkonen, Petri. "Jane Austen." *Author's Calendar*. Ed. Ari Pesonen. 2000. Last accessed 11 Nov. 2003. http://www.kirjasto.sci.fi/jausten.htm.
Biographical sketch and discussion of Austen's major works.

Matsuoka, Mitsuharu. *Jane Austen*. 28 Mar. 2001. Last accessed 11 Nov. 2003. http://lang.nagoya-u.ac.jp/~matsuoka/Austen.html.
An extensive list of links to Austen-related web sites.

Project Gutenberg. 25 Dec. 2003. Last accessed 27 Dec. 2003. http://www.gutenberg.net/index.shtml.

Includes online texts for several of Austen's works, including *Emma* and *Pride and Prejudice.* Use the "Find an Ebook" link to find texts by Austen.

The Republic of Pemberley. Last accessed 11 Nov. 2003. http://www.pemberley .com/.
   Extensive site on Austen's life, works, and culture.

Wilson, Sara. "The Persuasive and Provincial Jane Austen." *Literary Traveler.* Last accessed 11 Nov. 2003. http://www.literarytraveler.com/austen/jane austen.htm.
   Biographical profile of Austen.

Biographies and Criticism

Epstein, Julia. "Jane Austen." *Nineteenth-Century Literature Criticism* 119: 1–61.
   Discussion of life and works. Also includes a history of critical commentary on Austen's works.

Garcia-Johnson, Ronie-Richele. "Jane Austen." *Authors and Artists for Young Adults* 19: 1–11.
   Discussion of life, literary career, and influence.

Dictionaries, Encyclopedias, and Handbooks

Poplawski, Paul. *A Jane Austen Encyclopedia.* Westport, CT: Greenwood, 1998.
   Includes entries on various aspects of Austen's life and literary career.

AVI (WORTIS), 1937–

Web Sites

Avi. Last accessed 11 Nov. 2003. http://www.avi-writer.com/.
   Author web site. Includes biographical information.

"Avi." *Kidspace @ The Internet Public Library.* 1996. Last accessed 11 Nov. 2003. http://www.ipl.org/div/kidspace/askauthor/Avi.html.
   Interview with Avi.

"Avi." *Kidsreads.com.* Last accessed 11 Nov. 2003. http://www.kidsreads.com/ authors/au-avi.asp.
   Interview with Avi.

"Avi Bibliography." *Fantastic Fiction.* Last accessed 11 Nov. 2003. http://www .fantasticfiction.co.uk/authors/Avi.htm.
   List of Avi's major works.

"Featured Author: Avi." *Carol Hurst's Children's Literature Web Site.* 1999. Last accessed 11 Nov. 2003. http://www.carolhurst.com/authors/avi.html.
   Short biographical sketch; discussion of selected works by Avi.

Biographies and Criticism

"Avi." *Authors and Artists for Young Adults* 37: 7–17.
　Biographical sketch with portrait; discussion of Avi's works.

"Avi." *Children's Literature Review* 68: 1–46.
　Biographical sketch and discussion of major works; excerpts from reviews of Avi's works.

"Avi." *Something About the Author* 108: 5–13.
　Discusses Avi's life and major works.

Bloom, Susan P., and Cathryn M. Mercier. *Presenting Avi*. New York: Twayne Publishers, 1997.
　Critical commentary on Avi's works. Includes a secondary bibliography.

Sieruta, Peter D. "Avi." Silvey, *Children's Books and Their Creators*. 38–39.
　Biographical sketch.

Wilson, Nance S. "Avi (Wortis)." Cullinan and Person, *The Continuum Encyclopedia of Children's Literature*. 49–51.
　Biographical sketch.

WILBERT VERE AWDRY, 1911–1997

Web Sites

"The Origins of Thomas the Tank Engine." *Drew and Jamies *Unofficial* Thomas the Tank Engine Page*. Last accessed 11 Nov. 2003. http://www.iglobal.com/Drew/origins.htm.
　Discusses the Thomas the Tank Engine books. Some biographical information.

"Rev. W. V. Awdry 1911–1997 'Thomas's Only Begetter.'" *Awdry Family Web Site*. Last accessed 16 July 2004. http://www.aran48.dsl.pipex.com/wilbert.htm.
　Portrait; biographical information.

Biographies and Criticism

"Awdry, Wilbert Vere." *Something About the Author* 67: 14–15.
　Biographical profile, discussion of major works.

Dahlberg, M. Margaret. "Wilbert Vere Awdry." Hettinga and Schmidt, *British Children's Writers, 1914–1960* (*Dictionary of Literary Biography* 160): 19–23.
　Discussion of literary career and influence.

"W(ilbert) V(ere) A(wdry)." *Children's Literature Review* 23: 1–7.
　Biographical sketch; excerpts from reviews and literary criticism of Awdry's works.

NATALIE BABBITT, 1932–

Web Sites

Del Negro, Janice M. "True Blue: Natalie Babbitt." *The Bulletin of the Center for Children's Books.* 1 June 1999. Last accessed 11 Nov. 2003. http://alexia .lis.uiuc.edu/puboff/bccb/0699true.html.
 Short biographical article; list of major works.

Milner, Joseph O. "Hard Religious Questions in *Knee-Knock Rise* and *Tuck Everlasting.*" *ALAN Review* 22: 2 (Winter 1995). Last accessed 11 Nov. 2003. http://scholar.lib.vt.edu/ejournals/ALAN/winter95/Milner.html.
 Critical essay.

"Natalie Babbitt." *Kidspace @ The Internet Public Library.* 1996. Last accessed 11 Nov. 2003. http://www.ipl.org/div/kidspace/askauthor/babbitt.html.
 Short biographical article on Babbitt with portrait.

"Natalie Babbitt's Biography." *Scholastic.* Last accessed 11 Nov. 2003. http://www2 .scholastic.com/teachers/authorsandbooks/authorstudies/authorhome.jhtml? authorID=8&collateralID=5095&displayName=Biography.
 Short biography with portrait and links to an interview with Babbitt; bibliography.

Biographies and Criticism

Edwards, Eden. "Babbitt, Natalie." Silvey, *Children's Books and Their Creators.* 42–44.

Levy, Michael M. *Natalie Babbitt.* Boston: Twayne Publishers, 1991.
 Critical commentary on Babbitt's works.

Moss, Anita. "Natalie Babbitt." Estes, *American Writers for Children Since 1960: Fiction (Dictionary of Literary Biography* 52): 22–29.
 Discusses Babbitt's literary career and major works.

"Natalie Babbitt." *Authors and Artists for Young Adults* 51: 37–44.
 Biographical sketch with portrait; discussion of major works.

"Natalie (Zane Moore) Babbitt." *Children's Literature Review* 53: 20–39.
 Biographical sketch, discussion of major literary works, excerpts from reviews.

Bibliographies

"Babbitt, Natalie." Lynn, *Fantasy Literature Children and Young Adults.* 615–17.
 Lists books and articles about Babbitt and her works.

ENID BAGNOLD, 1889–1981

Web Sites

"Enid Bagnold." *CORAL (Caribbean Online Resource and Archive).* 2002. Last accessed 22 Dec. 2003. http://www.caribbeanedu.com/coral/refcen/ Biography/ readbio.asp?id=21.
Short biographical sketch.

"Enid Bagnold (1889–1981)." *Women of Brighton.* Last accessed 11 Nov. 2003. http://www.womenofbrighton.co.uk/enidbagnold.htm.
Short, biographical sketch, portrait, brief discussion of major works.

"Enid Bagnold Papers." *Yale University Beinecke Rare Book and Manuscript Library.* Dec. 1997. Last accessed 11 Nov. 2003. http://webtext.library.yale .edu/xml2html/beinecke.BAGNOLD.con.html.
Description of Enid Bagnold archival holdings at Yale University. Includes biographical sketch.

Biographies and Criticism

"Bagnold, Enid." *Something About the Author* 25: 23–34.
Biographical sketch and chronology. Primary and secondary bibliographies.

Broughton, Mary Ariail. "Bagnold, Enid." Cullinan and Person, *The Continuum Encyclopedia of Children's Literature.* 60.
Biographical sketch.

Donahue, Rosanne. "Enid Bagnold." Hettinga and Schmidt, *British Children's Writers, 1914-1960 (Dictionary of Literary Biography* 160): 24–29.
Discussion of literary career and influence.

Sieruta, Peter D. "Bagnold, Enid." Silvey, *Children's Books and Their Creators.* 44.
Biographical sketch.

R. M. BALLANTYNE, 1825–1894

Web Sites

"Life and Works of R. M. Ballantyne (1824–1894)." *Athelstane E-Texts.* 2003. Last accessed 11 Nov. 2003. http://www.athelstane.co.uk/ballanty/ballanty.htm.
Includes a biography and links to online full-text versions of selected works.

Liukkonen, Petri. "R. M. Ballantyne." *Author's Calendar.* Ed. Ari Pesonen. 2000. Last accessed 11 Nov. 2003. http://www.kirjasto.sci.fi/ballant.htm.
Biographical sketch and discussion of Ballantyne's major works.

Project Gutenberg. 25 Dec. 2003. Last accessed 27 Dec. 2003. http://www .gutenberg.net/index.shtml.
Includes online texts for a couple of Ballantyne's works, including *The Young Fur Traders* (use the "Find an Ebook" link to find texts by Ballantyne).

Biographies and Criticism

"Ballantyne, R(obert) M(ichael)." *Something About the Author* 24: 32–37.
    Biographical sketch, discussion of major works.

Chaston, Joel D. "R. M. Ballantyne." Khorana, *British Children's Writers,
    1800–1880 (Dictionary of Literary Biography* 163): 8–20.
    Discussion of literary career and influence.

Bibliographies

"Robert Michael Ballantyne." Rahn, *Children's Literature: An Annotated Bibliog-
    raphy of the History and Criticism.* 162–63.
    Lists books and articles about Ballantyne and his works.

J. M. BARRIE, 1860–1937

Web Sites

Birken, Andrew. *jmbarrie.co.uk.* 1 Nov. 2003. Last accessed 11 Nov. 2003.
    http://www.jmbarrie.co.uk/.
    Includes resources for studying Barrie.

"JM Barrie." *BBC Books.* Last accessed 11 Nov. 2003. http://www.bbc.co.uk/arts/
    books/author/barrie/.
    Portrait, biographical sketch, list of major works.

Liukkonen, Petri. "J. M. Barrie." *Author's Calendar.* Ed. Ari Pesonen. 2000. Last
    accessed 11 Nov. 2003. http://www.kirjasto.sci.fi/jmbarrie.htm.
    Biographical sketch and discussion of Barrie's major works.

MacRitchie, John."Sir J. M. Barrie." *Scottish Authors.* 1 July 2000. Last accessed
    11 Nov. 2003. http://www.slainte.org.uk/Scotauth/barridsw.htm.
    Short biographical sketch.

Project Gutenberg. 25 Dec. 2003. Last accessed 27 Dec. 2003. http://www
    .gutenberg.net/index.shtml.
    Includes uncopyrighted online texts for several of Barries's works, includ-
ing *Peter Pan* (use the "Find an Ebook" link to find texts by Barrie).

Biographies and Criticism

Amster, Mara Ilyse. "Barrie, Sir J. M." Silvey, *Children's Books and Their Cre-
    ators.* 46.
    Short biographical sketch.

"Barrie, J(ames) M(atthew)." *Something About the Author* 100: 13–18.
    Biographical profile.

Beasley, Denise P., and Janelle B. Mathis. "Barrie, J(ames) M(atthew)." Cullinan
    and Person, *The Continuum Encyclopedia of Children's Literature.* 63–64.
    Short biographical sketch.

"(Sir) J(ames) M(atthew) Barrie." *Children's Literature Review* 16: 1–40.
Biographical profile, discussion of major works, excerpts from reviews and literary criticism.

White, Donna R. "J. M. Barrie." Zaidman, *British Children's Writers, 1880–1914* (*Dictionary of Literary Biography* 141): 23–39.
Discussion of literary career and influence.

Bibliographies

"Barrie, J[ames] M[atthew]." Hendrickson, *Children's Literature: A Guide to the Criticism*. 23–24.
Lists books and articles about Barrie and his works.

"James Michael Barrie." Rahn, *Children's Literature: An Annotated Bibliography of the History and Criticism*. 166–69.
Lists books and articles about Barrie and his works.

L. FRANK BAUM, 1856–1919

Web Sites

Liukkonen, Petri. "L(yman) Frank Baum." *Author's Calendar.* Ed. Ari Pesonen. 2000. Last accessed 11 Nov. 2003. http://www.kirjasto.sci.fi/lfbaum.htm.
Biographical sketch and discussion of Baum's major works.

McGovern, Linda. "The Man Behind the Curtain: L. Frank Baum and the Wizard of Oz." *Literary Traveler.* Last accessed 11 Nov. 2003. http://www.literary traveler.com/spring/west/baum.htm.
Biographical sketch, portrait.

"The Oz Encyclopedia." *Piglet Press.* 10 May 2003. Last accessed 11 Nov. 2003. http://www.halcyon.com/piglet.
Includes biographical information on Baum and information about his Oz books.

Project Gutenberg. 25 Dec. 2003. Last accessed 27 Dec. 2003. http://www .gutenberg.net/index.shtml.
Includes uncopyrighted online texts for several of Baum's works, including *The Wizard of Oz* and *American Fairy Tales* (use the "Find an Ebook" link to find texts by Baum).

Biographies and Criticism

"Baum, L(yman) Frank." *Something About the Author* 100: 18–23.
Biographical sketch; discussion of major works.

"Frank Baum." *Twentieth-Century Literature Criticism* 132: 1–109.
Discussion of critical influence, extensive discussion of critical commentary on Baum.

Hearn, Michael Patrick. "L. Frank Baum." Cech, *American Writers for Children, 1900–1960* (*Dictionary of Literary Biography* 22): 13–36.
Discussion of Baum's literary career and influence.

"L(yman) Frank Baum." *Children's Literature Review* 15: 12–46.
Biographical sketch, discussion of literary career, excerpts from reviews and critical commentary.

Mathis, Janelle B. "Baum, L(yman) Frank." Cullinan and Person, *The Continuum Encyclopedia of Children's Literature.* 68–69.
Biographical sketch.

Rogers, Katharine M. *L. Frank Baum, Creator of Oz.* New York: St. Martin's Press, 2002.
Book-length biography of Baum. Includes discussion of his major works.

Bibliographies

"Baum, L[yman] Frank." Hendrickson, *Children's Literature: A Guide to the Criticism.* 25–27.
Lists books and articles about Baum and his works.

"Lyman Frank Baum." Rahn, *Children's Literature: An Annotated Bibliography of the History and Criticism.* 169–76.
Lists books and articles about Baum and his works.

NINA BAWDEN, 1925–

Web Sites

Nina Bawden and Her Books. Last accessed 11 Nov. 2003. http://www.nina bawden.net/.
Author web site. Information on Bawden's life and books.

"Nina Bawden Papers." *de Grummond Collection.* June 2001. Last accessed 11 Nov. 2003. http://www.lib.usm.edu/%7Edegrum/html/research/findaids/ bawden.htm.
Description of the Nina Bawden archival papers at the de Grummond Collection. Includes biographical sketch, discussion of major works.

Biographies and Criticism

"Bawden, Nina (Mary Mabey)." *Something About the Author* 72: 6–10.
Biographical sketch, discussion of major works.

"Nina (Mary Mabey) Bawden." *Children's Literature Review* 51: 1–43.
Biographical sketch, discussion of major works, excerpts from reviews.

Silbert, Martha F. "Bawden, Nina." Silvey, *Children's Books and Their Creators.* 50–51.
Biographical sketch.

Smith, Louisa. "Nina Bawden." Hunt, *British Children's Writers Since 1960* (*Dictionary of Literary Biography* 161): 20–28.
Discussion of literary career and influence.

JOHN BELLAIRS, 1938–1991

Web Sites

The Complete Bellairs. Ed. Jonathan Abucejo. Last accessed 15 Nov. 2003. http://www.compleatbellairs.com/.
Biographical information and discussion of Bellairs's works.

"John Bellairs Bibliography." *Fantastic Fiction.* Last accessed 15 Nov. 2003. http://www.fantasticfiction.co.uk/authors/John_Bellairs.htm.
List of Bellairs's major works.

John Bellairs: The Man, the Manuscripts and the Magic. Ed. Craig Seemann, Jon Shanks. 11 Nov. 2003. Last accessed 15 Nov. 2003. http://www.bellairsia .com/.
Biographical information, including a time line, discussion of Bellairs's works.

Biographies and Criticism

Broughton, Mary Ariail. "Bellairs, John." Cullinan and Person, *The Continuum Encyclopedia of Children's Literature.* 72–73.
Biographical sketch.

Des Chenes, Elizabeth A. "Bellairs, John." *Something About the Author* 68: 23–25.
Biographical sketch, discussion of major works.

"John Bellairs." *Children's Literature Review* 37: 1–29.
Biographical sketch, discussion of literary career, excerpts from reviews and literary criticism.

LUDWIG BEMELMANS, 1898–1962

Web Sites

"Bemelmans, Ludwig." *Educational Paperback Association.* Last accessed 15 Nov. 2003. http://www.edupaperback.org/showauth.cfm?authid=13.
Biographical sketch with list of major works.

"Madeline." *Kidsreads.com.* Last accessed 15 Nov. 2003. http://www.kidsreads .com/series/series-madeline-author.asp.
Biographical sketch; discussion of works. Also includes links to information about the Madeline series.

"Madeline." *Penguin Group USA.* 1998. Last accessed 15 Nov. 2003. http://www .penguinputnam.com/static/packages/us/yreaders/madeline/index.htm.

Publisher web site. Includes biographical sketch about Bemelmans and a written account by Bemelmans on the origin of the *Madeline* books.

Madeline.com. 2003. Last accessed 15 Nov. 2003. http://www.madeline.com/.
Official web site. Includes biographical sketch on Bemelmans.

Biographies and Criticism

"Bemelmans, Ludwig." *Something About the Author* 100: 24–27.
Biographical sketch, discussion of major works.

Eastman, Jacqueline Fisher. *Ludwig Bemelmans.* New York: Twayne Publishers, 1996.
Critical commentary on Bemelmans's works.

Ellinger, Marguerite. "Bemelmans, Ludwig." Cullinan and Person, *The Continuum Encyclopedia of Children's Literature.* 75–76.
Biographical sketch.

Jennerich, Edward J. "Ludwig Bemelmans." Cech, *American Writers for Children, 1900–1960 (Dictionary of Literary Biography* 22): 37–42.
Discussion of literary career and influence.

"Ludwig Bemelmans." *Children's Literature Review* 6: 57–76.
Biographical sketch, discussion of literary career, excerpts from reviews and literary criticism.

Bibliographies

"Bemelmans, Ludwig." Hendrickson, *Children's Literature: A Guide to the Criticism.* 30–31.
Lists books and articles about Bemelmans and his works.

JAN BERENSTAIN, 1923– , AND STAN BERENSTAIN, 1923–

Web Sites

Berenstain Bear Country. 2003. Last accessed 23 Dec. 2003. http://www.berenstainbears.com/.
Official web site for the Berenstain Bear books. Includes biographical information about the Berenstains.

"Berenstain, Jan and Stan." *Educational Paperback Association.* Last accessed 15 Nov. 2003. http://www.edupaperback.org/showauth.cfm?authid=14.
Biographical sketch with list of major works.

"Jan and Stan Berenstain." *Kidsreads.com.* 2003. Last accessed 15 Nov. 2003. http://www.kidsreads.com/authors/au-berenstain-jan-stan.asp.
Biographical profiles.

Biographies and Criticism

"Berenstain, Jan(ice)." *Something About the Author* 135: 21–30.
 Biographical sketch, discussion of major works.

"Berenstain, Stan(ley)." *Something About the Author* 135: 30–37.
 Biographical sketch, discussion of major works.

Horton, Nancy. "Berenstain, Stanley and Janice." Cullinan and Person, *The Continuum Encyclopedia of Children's Literature.* 77.
 Biographical sketch.

"Stan(ley) Berenstain, Jan(ice) Berenstain." *Children's Literature Review* 18: 22–32.
 Biographical sketch, discussion of literary career, excerpts from reviews and literary criticism.

FRANCESCA LIA BLOCK, 1962–

Web Sites

"Conversations: The Cool Block." *Writes of Passage: The Online Source for Teenagers.* 1996. http://www.writes.org/conversations/conver_2.html.
 Interview with Block.

Francesca Lia Block. Last accessed 15 Nov. 2003. http://www. francescaliablock .com/.
 Author web site. Includes biographical information.

"Francesca Lia Block on *The Rose and the Beast: Fairy Tales Retold.*" *Harper Childrens.com.* Last accessed 15 Nov. 2003. http://www.harperchildrens .com/hch/author/features/block/.
 Interview with Block from publisher web site.

Maughan, Shannon. "Author Profile: Francesca Lia Block." *Teenreads.com.* 2003. Last accessed 15 Nov. 2003. http://www.teenreads.com/authors/ au-block-francesca.asp.
 Biographical profile; discussion of major works.

Platzner, Rebecca. "Collage in Francesca Lia Block's Weetzie Bat Books." *ALAN Review* 25: 2 (Winter 1998). Last accessed 15 Nov. 2003. http://scholar.lib.vt .edu/ejournals/ALAN/winter98/platzner.html.
 Critical essay.

Biographies and Criticism

"Francesca Lia Block." *Children's Literature Review* 33: 25–33.
 Biographical sketch, discussion of literary career, excerpts from reviews and literary criticism.

Henning, Karen Lee. "Block, Francesca Lia." Silvey, *The Essential Guide to Children's Books and Their Creators.* 45.
 Biographical sketch.

Jones, J. Sydney, and Ken Cuthbertson. "Francesca Lia Block." *Authors and Artists for Young Adults* 34: 47–54.
Biographical sketch with portrait, discussion of major works.

JUDY BLUME, 1938–

Web Sites

"Audio Interview with Judy Blume." *Wired for Books.* Last accessed 15 Nov. 2003. http://wiredforbooks.org/judyblume/.
Audio file from 1984 interview with Blume.

"Author Profile: Judy Blume." *Teenreads.com.* 2003. Last accessed 15 Nov. 2003. http://www.teenreads.com/authors/au-blume-judy.asp.
Biographical profile; interview with Blume.

"The Fudge Books." *Kidsreads.com.* 2003. Last accessed 15 Nov. 2003. http://www.kidsreads.com/series/series-fudge-author.asp.
Photo; short biographical sketch. Includes links to information on individual books and characters.

Judy Blume's Home Base. 28 May 2003. Last accessed 15 Nov. 2003. http://www.judyblume.com/menu-main.html.
Author web site. Includes biographical information.

Biographies and Criticism

Garcia-Johnson, R. "Judy Blume." *Authors and Artists for Young Adults* 26: 7–17.
Biographical sketch with portrait; discussion of major works.

"Judy Blume." *Children's Literature Review* 69: 1–41.
Biographical sketch, discussion of literary career, excerpts from reviews and literary criticism.

Naylor, Alice Phoebe. "Judy Blume." Estes, *American Writers for Children since 1960 (Dictionary of Literary Biography* 52): 30–38.
Discussion of literary career and influence.

Sutherland, Zena. "Blume, Judy." Silvey, *The Essential Guide to Children's Books and Their Creators.* 47–49.
Biographical sketch.

Bibliographies

"Blume, Judy." Hendrickson, *Children's Literature: A Guide to the Criticism.* 33–35.
Lists works about Blume and her works.

ENID BLYTON, 1897–1968

Web Sites

"Audio Interviews: Enid Mary Blyton." *BBC*. Last accessed 15 Nov. 2003. http://www.bbc.co.uk/bbcfour/audiointerviews/profilepages/blytone1.shtml. Audio files from 1963 BBC four interview; brief biographical sketch.

"Enid Blyton." *BBC Books*. Last accessed 15 Nov. 2003. http://www.bbc.co.uk/arts/books/author/blyton/. Portrait; biographical sketch.

Liukkonen, Petri. "Enid Blyton." *Author's Calendar*. Ed. Ari Pesonen. 2000. Last accessed 15 Nov. 2003. http://www.kirjasto.sci.fi/eblyton.htm. Biographical sketch and discussion of Blyton's major works.

An Unofficial Enid Blyton Home Page. 10 Apr. 2003. Last accessed 15 Nov. 2003. http://www.btinternet.com/~ajarvis/blyton.htm. Includes biographical information about Blyton.

Biographies and Criticism

"Blyton, Enid (Mary)." *Something About the Author* 25: 48–61. Biographical sketch with portrait, discussion of major works.

"Enid Blyton." *Children's Literature Review* 31: 30–64. Biographical sketch, discussion of literary career, excerpts from reviews and commentary.

Hunt, Peter. "Enid Blyton." Hettinga and Schmidt, *British Children's Writers, 1914–1960* (*Dictionary of Literary Biography* 160): 50–71. Discussion of literary career and influence. Includes primary and secondary bibliographies.

Ray, Shelia. The Blyton phenomenon: *The Controversy Surrounding the World's Most Successful Children's Writer.* London: Deutsch, 1982. Book-length study of Blyton's life and literary career.

Serafin, Steven R. "Blyton, Enid." Cullinan and Person, *The Continuum Encyclopedia of Children's Literature.* 91–93. Biographical sketch.

Bibliographies

"Blyton, Enid." Hendrickson, *Children's Literature: A Guide to the Criticism.* 35–37. Lists books and articles about Blyton and her works.

"Enid Blyton." Rahn, *Children's Literature: An Annotated Bibliography of the History and Criticism.* 177–78. Lists books and articles about Blyton and her works.

MICHAEL BOND, 1926–

Web Sites

"Biography of Michael Bond." *Paddington Bear: The Official Website.* 2003. Last accessed 15 Nov. 2003. http://www.paddingtonbear.co.uk/en/1/fachismbo .mxs.
Biographical sketch; portrait.

"Michael Bond." *Paddington Bear Homepage.* Last accessed 15 Nov. 2003. http://www.cobweb.nl/wcoumans/padbond.htm.
Portrait; biographical information. Part of a larger site devoted to the Paddington Bear books.

"Michael Bond Papers." *de Grummond Collection.* June 2001. Last accessed 15 Nov. 2003. http://www.lib.usm.edu/%7Edegrum/html/research/findaids/ bond.htm.
Description of Michael Bond archival papers at the de Grummond Collection. Includes biographical sketch, discussion of major works.

Biographies and Criticism

Amster, Mara Ilyse. "Bond, Michael." Silvey, *Children's Books and Their Creators.* 69–71.
Biographical sketch.

"Bond, (Thomas) Michael." *Children's Literature Review* 1: 27–30.
Biographical sketch, discussion of literary career, excerpts from reviews and commentary.

"Bond, (Thomas) Michael." *Something About the Author* 58: 14–29.
Biographical sketch with portrait, discussion of major works.

Matthews, Charles E. "Michael Bond." Hunt, *British Children's Writers Since 1960 (Dictionary of Literary Biography* 161) 29–35.
Discussion of literary career and influence.

SUE ELLEN BRIDGERS, 1942–

Web Sites

Crews, Becky, Mary Blair, and Danielle Shapiro, with Kay E. Vandergrift. "Learning About Sue Bridgers." *Vandergrift's Children's Literature Page.* 20 Sept. 1996. Last accessed 15 Nov. 2003. http://www.scils.rutgers.edu/ ~kvander/bridgers.html.
Biographical sketch, list of selected works, secondary references.

Gregg, Gail P., and P. Sissi Carroll. " 'What's It Like to Be You?' A Conversation with Sue Ellen Bridgers." *ALAN Review* 27: 2 (Winter 1999). Last accessed 15 Nov. 2003. http://scholar.lib.vt.edu/ejournals/ALAN/fall99/gregg.html.
Interview with Bridgers.

Mitchell, Karen. "The 'Different Truth' for Women in Sue Ellen Bridgers' *Permanent Connections.*" *ALAN Review* 21: 3 (Spring 1994). Last accessed 15 Nov. 2003. http://scholar.lib.vt.edu/ejournals/ALAN/spring94/Mitchell.html. Critical essay.

Biographies and Criticism

Hipple, Theodore W. "Sue Ellen Bridgers." Estes, *American Writers for Children Since 1960: Fiction* (*Dictionary of Literary Biography* 52): 38–41.
Discussion of literary career and influence.

Jones, J. Sydney. "Bridgers, Sue Ellen." *Something About the Author* 90: 32–36.
Biographical sketch with portrait, discussion of major works.

Lieberman, Craig. "Bridgers, Sue Ellen." Cullinan and Person, *The Continuum Encyclopedia of Children's Literature.* 111.
Biographical sketch.

"Sue Ellen Bridgers." *Children's Literature Review* 18: 20–28.
Biographical sketch, discussion of literary career, excerpts from reviews and commentary.

RAYMOND BRIGGS, 1934–

Web Sites

"Raymond Briggs." *BBC Books.* Last accessed 15 Nov. 2003. http://www.bbc.co .uk/arts/books/author/briggs/index.shtml.
Portrait, biographical sketch, discussion of major works.

Biographies and Criticism

"Briggs, Raymond (Redvers)." *Something About the Author* 131: 26–31.
Biographical sketch with portrait, discussion of major works.

Clark, Bill. "Briggs, Raymond." Silvey, *The Essential Guide to Children's Books and Their Creators.* 57–58.
Biographical sketch.

"Raymond (Redvers) Briggs." *Children's Literature Review* 10: 15–36.
Biographical sketch, discussion of literary career, excerpts from reviews and commentary.

GWENDOLYN BROOKS, 1917–2000

Web Sites

"Gwendolyn Brooks." *Academy of American Poets.* 8 Feb. 2001. Last accessed 15 Nov. 2003. http://www.poets.org/poets/poets.cfm?45442B7C000C07030F.
Biographical sketch, selected bibliography, links to related sites.

"Gwendolyn Brooks." *Gwendolyn Brooks Cultural Center.* Last accessed 15 Nov. 2003. http://www.student.services.wiu.edu/gbcc/Forum.asp.
Biographical sketch.

Reuben, Paul P. "Chapter 10: Late Twentieth Century—Gwendolyn Brooks (1917–2000)." *PAL: Perspectives in American Literature—A Research and Reference Guide.* 9 Jan. 2003. Last accessed 15 Nov. 2003. http://www.csustan.edu/english/reuben/pal/chap10/brooks.html.
Includes primary and secondary bibliographies, portrait, links to related sites.

Sullivan, James. "Gwendolyn Brooks." *Modern American Poetry.* Last accessed 15 Nov. 2003. http://www.english.uiuc.edu/maps/poets/a_f/brooks/brooks.htm.
Includes a biographical sketch, discussion of various works, articles on Brooks's works, and links to related web sites.

Tongier, Brian Christopher, and Emily Christine Jacobson. "Gwendolyn Brooks." *Voices from the Gaps: Women Writers of Color.* 10 Dec. 1996. Last accessed 15 Nov. 2003. http://voices.cla.umn.edu/newsite/authors/BROOKSgwendolyn.htm.
Biographical sketch, discussion of Brooks's major works. Includes selected primary and secondary bibliographies.

Biographies and Criticism

Dunne, Jennifer E. "Brooks, Gwendolyn." Cullinan and Person, *The Continuum Encyclopedia of Children's Literature.* 117.
Biographical sketch.

"Gwendolyn Brooks." *Children's Literature Review* 27: 44–56.
Biographical sketch, discussion of literary career, excerpts from reviews and commentary.

"Gwendolyn Brooks." *Contemporary Literary Criticism* 125: 42–114.
Discussion of critical influence, extensive discussion of critical commentary on Brooks.

Jones, J. Sydney. "Gwendolyn Brooks." *Authors and Artists for Young Adults* 20: 51–61.
Biographical sketch with portrait, discussion of major works.

MARC BROWN, 1946–

Web Sites

Arthur Worldwide.com. Fall 2003. Last accessed 15 Nov. 2003. http://www.arthurworldwide.com/.
Official web site. Includes information about Brown and his books.

Bruns, Ann L. "Arthur." *Kidsreads.com.* 2003. Last accessed 15 Nov. 2003. http://www.kidsreads.com/series/series-arthur.asp.

Includes a biographical sketch of Brown and information about his Arthur books.

"Marc Brown." *Time Warner Bookmark*. Last accessed 15 Nov. 2003. http://www
.twbookmark.com/authors/26/224/index.html.
Publisher web site. Biographical sketch; list of books available from publisher.

Biographies and Criticism

"Brown, Marc." *Something About the Author* 80: 23–7.
Biographical sketch with portrait, discussion of major works.

Goldsmith, Francisca. "Brown, Marc." Cullinan and Person, *The Continuum Encyclopedia of Children's Literature*. 119–20.
Biographical sketch.

"Marc Brown." *Children's Literature Review* 29: 1–20.
Biographical sketch, discussion of literary career, excerpts from reviews and commentary.

MARGARET WISE BROWN, 1910–1952

Web Sites

"Brown, Margaret Wise." *Educational Paperback Association*. Last accessed 15 Nov. 2003. http://www.edupaperback.org/showauth.cfm?authid=17.
Biographical sketch with list of major works.

Margaret Wise Brown. Last accessed 15 Nov. 2003. http://www.margaretwise
brown.com/.
Official web site. Includes biographical sketch, portraits, primary and secondary bibliographies.

The Unofficial Margaret Wise Brown Web Site. Last accessed 15 Nov. 2003. http://persweb.direct.ca/ikhan/wisebrown/index.html.
Information on Brown's life and works.

Biographies and Criticism

"Brown, Margaret Wise." *Something About the Author* 100: 35–39.
Biographical sketch with portrait, discussion of major works.

Marcus, Leonard S. "Brown, Margaret Wise." Silvey, *The Essential Guide to Children's Books and Their Creators*. 63–66.
Biographical sketch.

———. *Margaret Wise Brown: Awakened by the Moon*. Boston: Beacon Press, 1992.
Biographical sketch.

————. "Margaret Wise Brown." Cech, *American Writers for Children, 1900–1960* (*Dictionary of Literary Biography* 22) 42–70.
Discussion of literary career and influence.

"Margaret Wise Brown." *Children's Literature Review* 10: 37–69.
Biographical sketch, discussion of literary career, excerpts from reviews and commentary.

Bibliographies

"Brown, Margaret Wise." Hendrickson, *Children's Literature: A Guide to the Criticism.* 45.
List of books and articles about Brown and her works.

JOSEPH BRUCHAC, 1942–

Web Sites

Dresang, Eliza T. "An Interview with Joseph Bruchac." *Cooperative Children's Book Center, School of Education, University of Wisconsin-Madison.* Last accessed 23 Dec. 2003. http://www.education.wisc.edu/ccbc/bruchac.htm.
Transcript from a 1999 interview with Bruchac.

"Joseph Bruchac." *Penguin Group (USA).* 2000. Last accessed 23 Dec. 2003. http://www.penguinputnam.com/Author/AuthorFrame?0000003355.
Biographical sketch.

"Meet the Author: Joseph Bruchac." *Houghton Mifflin.* 2000. Last accessed 23 Dec. 2003. http://www.eduplace.com/kids/hmr/mtai/bruchac.html.
Biographical sketch.

Biographies and Criticism

"Bruchac, Joseph (III)." *Something About the Author* 131: 31–38.
Biographical sketch with portrait, discussion of major works.

"Joseph Bruchac, III." *Children's Literature Review* 46: 1–24.
Biographical sketch, discussion of literary career, excerpts from reviews and commentary.

Mathis, Janelle B. "Bruchac, Joseph." Cullinan and Person, *The Continuum Encyclopedia of Children's Literature.* 125–26.
Biographical sketch.

EVE BUNTING, 1928–

Web Sites

Cary, Alice. "A Talk with Eve Bunting: From the Titanic to Ancient Egypt." *BookPage*. 1997. Last accessed 15 Nov. 2003. http://www.bookpage.com/9705bp/childrens/evebunting.html.
Interview with Bunting.

"Eve Bunting." *Kidsreads.com*. Last accessed 15 Nov. 2003. http://www.kidsreads.com/authors/au-bunting-eve.asp.
Biographical sketch.

Biographies and Criticism

"Eve Bunting." *Children's Literature Review* 82: 1–53.
Biographical sketch, discussion of literary career, excerpts from reviews and commentary.

Greenlee, Adele. "Bunting, Eve." Cullinan and Person, *The Continuum Encyclopedia of Children's Literature*. 128–30.
Senick, Gerard J. "Bunting, (Anne) Eve(lyn)." *Something About the Author* 110: 26–34.
Biographical sketch with portrait, discussion of major works.

FRANCES HODGSON BURNETT, 1849–1924

Web Sites

"Frances Hodgson Burnett." *BBC Books*. Last accessed 15 Nov. 2003. http://www.bbc.co.uk/arts/books/author/burnett/index.shtml.
Biographical sketch; discussion of major works.

"Frances Hodgson Burnett." *CORAL (Caribbean Online Resource and Archive)*. 2002. Last accessed 22 Dec. 2003. http://www.caribbeanedu.com/coral/refcen/Biography/readbio.asp?id=33.
Biographical sketch.

"Frances Hodgson Burnett Bibliography." *Fantastic Fiction*. Last accessed 15 Nov. 2003. http://www.fantasticfiction.co.uk/authors/Frances_Hodgson_Burnett.htm.
List of Burnett's major works.

Project Gutenberg. 25 Dec. 2003. Last accessed 27 Dec. 2003. http://www.gutenberg.net/index.shtml.
Includes uncopyrighted online texts for several of Burnett's works, including *The Little Princess* and *The Secret Garden* (use the "Find an Ebook" link to find texts by Burnett).

Biographies and Criticism

Bixler, Phyllis. "Frances Hodgson Burnett." Estes, *American Writers for Children Before 1960: Fiction (Dictionary of Literary Biography* 42): 97–117.
Discussion of literary career and influence.

Burgess, Susan A. "Burnett, Frances Hodgson." Silvey, *Children's Books and Their Creators*. 105–6.
Biographical sketch.

"Burnett, Frances (Eliza) Hodgson." *Something About the Author* 100: 39–45.
Biographical sketch with portrait, discussion of major works.

"Frances Hodgson Burnett." *Children's Literature Review* 24: 21–60.
Biographical sketch, discussion of literary career, excerpts from reviews and commentary.

"Frances Hodgson Burnett." Hunt, *Four Writers for Children, 1868–1918: An Illustrated Chronicle (Dictionary of Literary Biography Documentary Series* 14): 95–148.
Discussion of literary career. Includes portraits.

Rutherford, L. M. "Frances Hodgson Burnett." Zaidman, *British Children's Writers, 1880–1914 (Dictionary of Literary Biography* 141): 59–78.
Discussion of literary career and influence.

Thwaite, Ann. *Waiting for the Party: The Life of Frances Hodgson Burnett, 1849–1924*. New York, Scribner, 1974.
Book-length study of Burnett's life and literary career.

Bibliographies

"Burnett, Frances Hodgson." Hendrickson, *Children's Literature: A Guide to the Criticism*. 50–52.
Lists books and essays about Burnett and her works.

"Frances Hodgson Burnett." Rahn, *Children's Literature: An Annotated Bibliography of the History and Criticism*. 184–86.
Lists books and articles about Burnett and her works.

VIRGINIA LEE BURTON, 1909–1968

Web Sites

"Mike Mulligan and His Steam Shovel." *Houghton Mifflin*. 2003. Last accessed 15 Nov. 2003. http://www.houghtonmifflinbooks.com/features/mike_mulligan/.
From publisher web site. Includes biographical information about Burton.

Mitts-Smith, Debra. "Gone but Not Forgotten: Virginia Lee Burton." *Bulletin of the Center for Children's Books*. 1 Aug. 2003. Last accessed 15 Nov. 2003. http://alexia.lis.uiuc.edu/puboff/bccb/0803focus.html.

Feature piece from the Bulletin of the Center for Children's Books. Discusses her major works and includes a list of them.

Ortakales, Denise. "Virginia Lee Burton." *Women Children's Book Illustrators.*
24 Aug. 2002. Last accessed 27 Dec. 2003. http://www.ortakales.com/
illustrators/.
Biographical sketch.

Biographies and Criticism

"Burton, Virginia Lee." *Something About the Author* 100: 45–47.
Biographical sketch with portrait, discussion of major works.

Kingman, Lee. "Burton, Virginia Lee." Silvey, *The Essential Guide to Children's
Books and Their Creators.* 71–72.
Biographical sketch.

Stott, Jon C. "Virginia Lee Burton." Cech, *American Writers for Children,
1900–1960* (*Dictionary of Literary Biography* 22): 88–94.
Discussion of literary career and influence.

"Virginia Lee Burton (Demetrios)." *Children's Literature Review* 11: 32–53.
Biographical sketch, discussion of literary career, excerpts from reviews
and commentary.

BETSY BYARS, 1928–

Web Sites

"Betsy Byars." *McDougal-Littell.* Last accessed 15 Nov. 2003. http://www
.mcdougallittell.com/disciplines/_lang_arts/authors/byars.cfm.
Publisher web site. Portrait; biographical profile.

"Betsy Byars." *Random House.* Last accessed 15 Nov. 2003. http://www
.randomhouse.com/teachers/authors/byar.html.
Publisher web site. Portrait; biographical profile.

"Betsy Byars Papers." *de Grummond Collection.* June 2001. Last accessed
15 Nov. 2003. http://www.lib.usm.edu/%7Edegrum/html/research/findaids/
byars.htm.
Description of Betsy Byars archival papers at the de Grummond Collection.
Includes biographical sketch, discussion of major works.

Callaway-Schaefer, Judith. "Betsy Byars: Techniques and Themes." *ALAN Review*
25: 1 (Fall 1997). Last accessed 15 Nov. 2003. http://scholar.lib.vt.edu/
ejournals/ALAN/fall97/schaefer.html.
Critical essay.

www.BetsyByars.com. 2003. Last accessed 15 Nov. 2003. http://www.betsybyars
.com/.
Author web site. Includes biographical information.

Biographies and Criticism

"Betsy Byars." *Children's Literature Review* 72: 1–22.
Biographical sketch, discussion of literary career, excerpts from reviews and commentary.

Reicha, Suan. "Betsy Byars." *Authors and Artists for Young Adults* 19: 63–74.
Biographical sketch with portrait, discussion of major works.

Segal, Elizabeth. "Betsy Byars." Estes, *American Writers for Children Since 1960: Fiction* (*Dictionary of Literary Biography* 52): 52–66.
Discussion of literary career and influence.

Usrey, Malcolm. *Betsy Byars*. New York: Twayne Publishers, 1995.
Discusses Byars's literary career and works.

Wilson, Nance S. "Byars, Betsy." Cullinan and Person, *The Continuum Encyclopedia of Children's Literature*. 136–37.
Biographical sketch.

Bibliographies

"Byars, Betsy (Cromer)." Lynn, *Fantasy Literature for Children and Young Adults*. 647–48.
Lists books and articles about Byars and her works.

MEG CABOT, 1967–

Web Sites

"Author Tracker: Meg Cabot." *HarperCollins*. Last accessed 23 Dec. 2003. http://www.harpercollins.com/catalog/author_xml.asp?AuthorId=19546.
Biographical sketch from publisher web site.

Meg Cabot. Last accessed 23 Dec. 2003. http://www.megcabot.com/.
Author's home page. Includes biographical information.

Biographies and Criticism

"Meg Cabot." *Authors and Artists for Young Adults* 50: 19–23.
Biographical sketch with portrait, discussion of major works.

"Meg Cabot." *Children's Literature Review* 85: 53–61.
Biographical sketch, discussion of literary career, excerpts from reviews and commentary.

ERIC CARLE, 1929–

Web Sites

Eric Carle. Last accessed 15 Nov. 2003. http://www.eric-carle.com/.
Author web site. Includes biographical information.

"Eric Carle." *Children's Book Council.* Last accessed 15 Nov. 2003. http://www.cbcbooks.org/html/ericcarle.html.
Biographical profile.

"Eric Carle." *Penguin.* Last accessed 15 Nov. 2003. http://www.penguinputnam.com/Author/AuthorFrame?0000030404.
Publisher web site. Biographical sketch with links to interview, list of books available from publisher.

Rouleau, Sandy, and Wendy Buchberg. "Eric Carle Author Study." *Scholastic.* Last accessed 15 Nov. 2003. http://teacher.scholastic.com/lessonrepro/lessonplans/ecarle.htm.
Publisher web site. Biographical piece, list of major works, lesson plan ideas.

Biographies and Criticism

"Eric Carle." *Children's Literature Review* 72: 49–62.
Biographical sketch, discussion of literary career, excerpts from reviews and commentary.

Jones, J. Sydney. "Carle, Eric." *Something About the Author* 120: 33–40.
Biographical sketch with portrait, discussion of major works.

Loer, Stephanie. "Carle, Eric." Silvey, *The Essential Guide to Children's Books and Their Creators.* 75–76.
Biographical sketch.

LEWIS CARROLL. *SEE* CHARLES LUTWIDGE DODGSON

LYDIA MARIA CHILD, 1802–1880

Web Sites

Project Gutenberg. 25 Dec. 2003. Last accessed 27 Dec. 2003. http://www.gutenberg.net/index.shtml.
Includes online texts for a couple of Child's works, including *The Magician's Show Box and Other Stories* (use the "Find an Ebook" link to find texts by Child).

Reuben, Paul P. "Chapter 4: Early Nineteenth Century—Lydia Maria Child (1802–1880)." *PAL: Perspectives in American Literature—A Research and Reference Guide.* 6 Jan. 2003. Last accessed 16 Nov. 2003. http://www.csustan.edu/english/reuben/pal/chap4/child.html.
Includes primary and secondary bibliographies, portrait, links to related sites.

Biographies and Criticism

"Child, Lydia Maria." *Something About the Author* 67: 46–51.
Biographical sketch with portrait, discussion of major works.

Joel, Patricia. "Child, Lydia Maria." Cullinan and Person, *The Continuum Encyclopedia of Children's Literature*. 163.
Biographical sketch.

"Lydia Marie Child." *Nineteenth-Century Literature Criticism* 73: 36–139.
Discussion of literary career; extensive discussion of critical commentary regarding Child's works.

JOHN CHRISTOPHER, 1922–

Web Sites

"John Christopher." *CORAL (Caribbean Online Resource and Archive)*. 2002. Last accessed 22 Dec. 2003. http://www.caribbeanedu.com/coral/refcen/Biography/readbio.asp?id=43.
Biographical sketch.

"John Christopher's Life and Works." *The Tripods*. Last accessed 16 Nov. 2003. http://www.gnelson.demon.co.uk/tripage/jc.html.
Portrait, biography, list of selected works.

Biographies and Criticism

"Christopher, John." *Children's Literature Review* 2: 37–44.
Biographical sketch, discussion of literary career, excerpts from reviews and commentary.

Pfeiffer, John R. "Christopher, John (Sam Youd)." Harris-Fain, *British Fantasy and Science-Fiction Writers, 1918–1960* (*Dictionary of Literary Biography* 255): 14–29.
Discussion of literary career and influence.

Shelton, Pamela L. "John Christopher." *Authors and Artists for Young Adults* 22: 15–23.
Biographical sketch with portrait, discussion of major works.

JOHN CIARDI, 1916–1986

Web Sites

"John Ciardi." *Academy of American Poets*. 3 Mar. 2001. Last accessed 16 Nov. 2003. http://www.poets.org/poets/poets.cfm?prmID=697.
Biographical sketch, selected bibliography, links to related sites.

Biographies and Criticism

"Ciardi, John." *Something About the Author* 65: 46–51.
   Biographical sketch with portrait, discussion of major works.

"John (Anthony) Ciardi." *Children's Literature Review* 19: 71–81.
   Biographical sketch, discussion of literary career, excerpts from reviews and commentary.

Phinney, Margaret Yatsevitch. "Ciardi, John." Cullinan and Person, *The Continuum Encyclopedia of Children's Literature*. 168–79.
   Biographical sketch.

SANDRA CISNEROS, 1954–

Web Sites

"Audio Interview with Sandra Cisneros." *Wired for Books*. Last accessed 16 Nov. 2003. http://wiredforbooks.org/sandracisneros/.
   Audio file from 1991 interview with Cisneros.

Juffer, Jane. "Sandra Cisneros." *Modern American Poetry*. Last accessed 16 Nov. 2003. http://www.english.uiuc.edu/maps/poets/a_f/cisneros/cisneros.htm.
   Includes a biographical sketch, discussion of various works, articles on Cisneros' works, and links to related web sites.

Mathias, Kelly. "Sandra Cisneros." *Voices from the Gaps: Women Writers of Color*. 26 Dec. 1996. Last accessed 16 Nov. 2003. http://voices.cla.umn.edu/newsite/authors/CISNEROSsandra.htm.
   Biographical sketch, discussion of Cisneros's major works. Includes selected primary and secondary bibliographies.

Reuben, Paul P. "Chapter 10: Late Twentieth Century—Sandra Cisneros (1954–   )." *PAL: Perspectives in American Literature—A Research and Reference Guide*. 9 Jan. 2003. Last accessed 16 Nov. 2003. http://www.csustan.edu/english/reuben/pal/chap10/cisneros.html.
   Includes primary and secondary bibliographies, portrait, links to related sites.

"Sandra Cisneros." *Academy of American Poets*. 17 July 2001. Last accessed 16 Nov. 2003. http://www.poets.org/poets/poets.cfm?prmID=766.
   Biographical sketch, selected bibliography, links to related sites.

Biographies and Criticism

Elias, Eduardo F. "Sandra Cisneros." Lomeli, Francisco A., and Carl R. Shirley, eds. *Chicano Writers, Second Series* (*Dictionary of Literary Biography* 122): 77–81. Detroit, MI: Gale, 1992.
   Discussion of literary career and influence.

Horton, Nancy. "Cisneros, Sandra." Cullinan and Person, *The Continuum Encyclopedia of Children's Literature*. 169.
   Biographical sketch.

"Sandra Cisneros." *Authors and Artists for Young Adults* 53: 43–52.
Biographical sketch with portrait, discussion of major works.

BEVERLY CLEARY, 1916–

Web Sites

"Beverly Cleary." *CORAL (Caribbean Online Resource and Archive)*. 2002. Last
accessed 22 Dec. 2003. http://www.caribbeanedu.com/coral/refcen/Bio
graphy/readbio.asp?id=45.
Biographical sketch.

"Beverly Cleary." *Kidsreads.com*. Last accessed 16 Nov. 2003. http://www.kids
reads.com/authors/au-cleary-beverly.asp.
Biographical profile.

Drennan, Miriam. "I Can See Cleary Now." *BookPage*. 1999. Last accessed 16
Nov. 2003. http://www.bookpage.com/9908bp/beverly_cleary.html.
Interview with Cleary.

The World of Beverly Cleary. Last accessed 16 Nov. 2003. http://www.beverly
cleary.com/.
Author web site. Includes biographical information.

Biographies and Criticism

"Beverly Cleary." *Children's Literature Review* 72: 63–151.
Biographical sketch, discussion of literary career, excerpts from reviews
and commentary.

Cleary, Beverly. *A Girl from Yamhill: A Memoir*. New York: Morrow, 1988.
Autobiography.

Pflieger, Pat. *Beverly Cleary*. Boston: Twayne Publishers, 1991.
Discusses Cleary's literary career and works.

Senick, Gerard J. "Cleary, Beverly." *Something About the Author* 121: 50–62.
Biographical sketch with portrait, discussion of major works.

Sieruta, Peter D. "Cleary, Beverly." Silvey, *The Essential Guide to Children's
Books and Their Creators*. 89–90.
Biographical sketch.

Trout, Anita. "Beverly Cleary." Estes, *American Writers for Children Since 1960:
Fiction (Dictionary of Literary Biography* 52): 84–91.
Discussion of literary career and influence.

Bibliographies

"Cleary, Beverly (Atlee Bunn)." Lynn, *Fantasy Literature for Children and Young
Adults*. 666–67.
Lists books and articles about Cleary and her works.

SAMUEL LANGHORNE CLEMENS (MARK TWAIN), 1835–1910

Web Sites

Liukkonen, Petri. "Mark Twain." *Author's Calendar*. Ed. Ari Pesonen. 2000. Last accessed 13 Dec. 2003. http://www.kirjasto.sci.fi/mtwain.htm.
Biographical sketch and discussion of Clemens's major works.

Project Gutenberg. 25 Dec. 2003. Last accessed 27 Dec. 2003. http://www .gutenberg.net/index.shtml.
Includes online texts for several of Clemens's works, including *The Adventures of Tom Sawyer* (use the "Find an Ebook" link to find texts by Clemens).

Reuben, Paul P. "Chapter 5: Late Nineteenth Century—Mark Twain (1835–1910)." *PAL: Perspectives in American Literature—A Research and Reference Guide*. 30 Oct. 2003. Last accessed 12 Dec. 2003. http://www.csustan.edu/english/reuben/pal/chap5/twain.html.
Includes primary and secondary bibliographies, portrait, links to related sites.

Biographies and Criticism

Barclay, Donald A. "Twain, Mark." Silvey, *The Essential Guide to Children's Books and Their Creators*. 451–53.
Biographical sketch.

"Clemens, Samuel Langhorne." *Something About the Author* 100: 52–62.
Biographical sketch with portrait, discussion of major works.

"Mark Twain." *Children's Literature Review* 58: 144–83.
Biographical sketch, discussion of literary career, excerpts from reviews and commentary about Clemens's *The Adventures of Tom Sawyer*.

Dictionaries, Encyclopedias, and Handbooks

LeMaster, J. R., James D. Wilson, and Christie Graves Hamric. *Mark Twain Encyclopedia*. New York: Garland, 1993.
Includes entries on various aspects of Clemens's life and literary career.

Rasmussen, R. Kent. *Mark Twain A to Z: The Essential Reference to His Life and Writings*. New York: Facts on File, 1995.
Includes entries on various aspects of Clemens's life and literary career.

Bibliographies

"Mark Twain." Rahn, *Children's Literature: An Annotated Bibliography of the History and Criticism*. 364–73.
Lists books and articles about Clemens and his works.

"Twain, Mark [Samuel L. Clemens]." Hendrickson, *Children's Literature: A Guide to the Criticism*. 276–77.
Lists books and articles about Clemens and his works.

LUCILLE CLIFTON, 1936–

Web Sites

Grischkowsky, Angela, Heidi Hemmen, and Jason Schindler. "Lucille Clifton." *Voices from the Gaps: Women Writers of Color*. 9 Sept. 1998. Last accessed 16 Nov. 2003. http://voices.cla.umn.edu/newsite/authors/CLIFTONlucille .htm.
Biographical sketch; discussion of Clifton's major works. Includes selected primary and secondary bibliographies.

"Lucille Clifton." *Academy of American Poets*. 16 Nov. 2000. Last accessed 16 Nov. 2003. http://www.poets.org/poets/poets.cfm?prmID=80.
Biographical sketch, selected bibliography, links to related sites.

Reuben, Paul P. "Chapter 10: Late Twentieth Century—Lucille Clifton (1936–)." *PAL: Perspectives in American Literature—A Research and Reference Guide*. 9 Jan. 2003. Last accessed 16 Nov. 2003. http://www.csustan.edu/english/ reuben/pal/chap10/clifton.html.
Includes primary and secondary bibliographies, portrait, links to related sites.

Biographies and Criticism

Ash, Gwynne Ellen. "Clifton, Lucille." Cullinan and Person, *The Continuum Encyclopedia of Children's Literature*. 179–80.
Biographical sketch.

"Clifton, (Thelma) Lucille." *Something About the Author* 128: 46–52.
Biographical sketch with portrait, discussion of major works.

"Lucille Clifton." *Children's Literature Review* 5: 51–60.
Biographical sketch, discussion of literary career, excerpts from reviews and commentary.

Peppers, Wallace R. "Lucille Clifton." Harris, Trudier, and Thadious M. Davis, eds. *Afro-American Poets Since 1955* (*Dictionary of Literary Biography* 41): 55–64. Detroit, MI: Gale, 1985.
Discussion of Clifton's life and literary career.

ELIZABETH COATSWORTH, 1893–1986

Web Sites

"Elizabeth Coatsworth." *Old Children's Books*. Last accessed 16 Nov. 2003. http://www.oldchildrensbooks.com/coatsworth.php.
Biographical sketch from book-dealer site.

"Elizabeth Coatsworth Papers." *de Grummond Collection*. 30 May 2001. Last accessed 16 Nov. 2003. http://www.lib.usm.edu/%7Edegrum/html/research/ findaids/coatswor.htm.

Description of Elizabeth Coatsworth archival papers at the de Grummond Collection. Includes biographical sketch, discussion of major works.

"Elizabeth Coatsworth Papers." *University of Delaware Library Special Collections Department*. 10 Mar. 2003. Last accessed 16 Nov. 2003. http://www.lib.udel.edu/ud/spec/findaids/coats.htm.
Description of Elizabeth Coatsworth archival papers at the University of Delaware. Includes biographical sketch.

Biographies and Criticism

"Coatsworth, Elizabeth." *Children's Literature Review* 2: 51–64.
Biographical sketch, discussion of literary career, excerpts from reviews and commentary.

"Coatsworth, Elizabeth." *Something About the Author* 100: 62–67.
Biographical sketch with portrait, discussion of major works.

Hamilton, Annalee. "Coatsworth, Elizabeth." Cullinan and Person, *The Continuum Encyclopedia of Children's Literature*. 181.
Biographical sketch.

Lukens, Rebecca. "Elizabeth Coatsworth." Cech, *American Writers for Children, 1900–1960* (*Dictionary of Literary Biography* 22): 94–102.
Discussion of literary career and influence.

Bibliographies

"Coatsworth, Elizabeth." Hendrickson, *Children's Literature: A Guide to the Criticism*. 70–71.
Lists books and articles about Coatsworth and her works.

CARLO COLLODI, 1826–1890

Web Sites

"Carlo Collodi." *Library*. Last accessed 16 Nov. 2003. http://www.ricochet-jeunes.org/eng/biblio/author/collodi.html.
Brief biographical sketch.

Liukkonen, Petri. "Carlo Collodi." *Author's Calendar*. Ed. Ari Pesonen. 2000. Last accessed 16 Nov. 2003. http://www.kirjasto.sci.fi/collodi.htm.
Biographical sketch and discussion of Collodi's major works.

Project Gutenberg. 25 Dec. 2003. Last accessed 27 Dec. 2003. http://www.gutenberg.net/index.shtml.
Includes an uncopyrighted online text for Collodi's *Adventures of Pinocchio* (use the "Find an Ebook" link to find text).

"The Story of Pinocchio." *Your Way to Florence*. Last accessed 16 Nov. 2003. http://www.arca.net/db/pinocchio/pinocchio.htm.
Brief biographical sketch.

Biographies and Criticism

Burgess, Susan A. "Collodi, Carlo." Silvey, *The Essential Guide to Children's Books and Their Creators*. 96–97.
　　Biographical sketch.

"Carlo Collodi." *Children's Literature Review* 5: 69–87.
　　Biographical sketch, discussion of literary career, excerpts from reviews and commentary.

"Lorenzini, Carlo." *Something About the Author* 100: 163–65.
　　Biographical sketch with portrait, discussion of major works.

Bibliographies

"Carlo Collodi." Rahn, *Children's Literature: An Annotated Bibliography of the History and Criticism*. 202–3.
　　Lists books and articles about Collodi and his works.

"Collodi, Carlo (Carlo Lorenzini)." Hendrickson, *Children's Literature: A Guide to the Criticism*. 71–73.
　　Lists books and articles about Collodi and his works.

BARBARA COONEY, 1917–2000

Web Sites

"Barbara Cooney Papers." *de Grummond Collection*. 4 Mar. 1996. Last accessed 16 Nov. 2003. http://www.lib.usm.edu/%7Edegrum/html/research/findaids/cooney.htm.
　　Description of Barbara Cooney archival papers at the de Grummond Collection. Includes biographical sketch, discussion of major works.

"Beads on a String: The Art of Barbara Cooney." *University of Connecticut Libraries Exhibitions*. Last accessed 16 Nov. 2003. http://www.lib.uconn.edu/about/exhibits/cooney/conyfpg.htm.
　　Includes a biographical sketch.

"Featured Author: Barbara Cooney." *Carol Hurst's Children's Literature Web Site*. 1999. Last accessed 16 Nov. 2003. http://www.carolhurst.com/authors/bcooney.html.
　　Short biographical sketch, discussion of selected works by Cooney.

Biographies and Criticism

"Barbara Cooney." *Children's Literature Review* 23: 15–33.
　　Biographical sketch, discussion of literary career, excerpts from reviews and commentary.

Mathis, Janelle B. "Cooney, Barbara." Cullinan and Person, *The Continuum Encyclopedia of Children's Literature*. 193–95.
　　Biographical sketch.

Senick, Gerard J. "Cooney, Barbara." *Something About the Author* 96: 67–75.
Biographical sketch with portrait, discussion of major works.

CAROLINE COONEY, 1947–

Web Sites

"Caroline B. Cooney Bibliography." *Fantastic Fiction*. Last accessed 16 Nov. 2003. http://www.fantasticfiction.co.uk/authors/Caroline_B_Cooney.htm.
Lists Cooney's major works.

"Caroline Cooney." *Kidsread.com*. Last accessed 16 Nov. 2003. http://www.kids reads.com/authors/au-cooney-caroline.asp.
Photo and autobiographical sketch.

Grand, Dee Ann. "Interview with Caroline Cooney." *BookPage*. Last accessed 16 Nov. 2003. http://www.bookpage.com/9611bp/childrens/thevoiceontheradio .html.
Portrait, interview, discussion of recent works.

Biographies and Criticism

Telgen, Diane. "Caroline B. Cooney." *Authors and Artists for Young Adults* 32: 23–32.
Biographical sketch with portrait, discussion of major works.

Wilson, Nance S. "Cooney, Caroline." Cullinan and Person, *The Continuum Encyclopedia of Children's Literature*. 195.
Biographical sketch.

SUSAN COOPER, 1935–

Web Sites

Scott, Mark. *The Lost Land*. 10 Aug. 2003. Last accessed 24 Nov. 2003. http://www.thelostland.com.htm.
Includes a biographical sketch and information about Cooper's major works.

"Susan Cooper." *CORAL (Caribbean Online Resource and Archive)*. 2002. Last accessed 22 Dec. 2003. http://www.caribbeanedu.com/coral/refcen/ Biography/readbio.asp?id=50.
Biographical sketch.

"Susan Cooper." *Kidsreads.com*. Last accessed 24 Nov. 2003. http://www.kids reads.com/authors/au-cooper-susan.asp.
Autobiographical sketch.

"Susan Cooper Bibliography." *Fantastic Fiction*. Last accessed 24 Nov. 2003. http://www.fantasticfiction.co.uk/authors/Susan_Cooper.htm.
Lists Cooper's major works.

Biographies and Criticism

Chaston, Joel D. "Susan Cooper." Hunt, *British Children's Writers Since 1960* (*Dictionary of Literary Biography* 161): 69–82.
Discussion of literary career and influence.

Horton, Nancy. "Cooper, Susan." Cullinan and Person, *The Continuum Encyclopedia of Children's Literature*. 196–97.
Biographical sketch.

Mikkelsen, Nina. *Susan Cooper*. New York: Twayne Publishers, 1998.
Critical commentary on Cooper's works.

Senick, Gerard J. "Cooper, Susan." *Something About the Author* 104: 28–38.
Biographical sketch with portrait, discussion of major works.

"Susan Cooper." *Children's Literature Review* 67: 1–24.
Biographical sketch, discussion of literary career, excerpts from reviews and commentary.

Bibliographies

"Cooper (Grant), Susan (Mary)." Lynn, *Fantasy Literature for Children and Young Adults*. 672–74.
Lists books and articles about Cooper and her works.

ROBERT CORMIER, 1925–2000

Web Sites

"Author Profile: Robert Cormier." *Teenreads.com*. Last accessed 24 Nov. 2003. http://www.teenreads.com/authors/au-cormier-robert.asp.
Interview with Cormier.

"Cormier, Robert." *Kidspace @ The Internet Public Library*. Last accessed 24 Nov. 2003. http://ipl.sils.umich.edu/div/kidspace/askauthor/Cormier.html.
Short biographical article with portrait.

Gardner, Lyn. "Dead Bodies in Suburbia." *Guardian Unlimited*. 19 Aug. 2000. Last accessed 24 Nov. 2003. http://books.guardian.co.uk/departments/childrenandteens/story/0,6000,355908,00.html.
Interview with Cormier.

Headley, Kathy Neal. "Duel at High Noon: A Replay of Cormier's Works." *ALAN Review* 20: 2 (Winter 1994). Last accessed 24 Nov. 2003. http://scholar.lib.vt.edu/ejournals/ALAN/winter94/Headley.html.
Critical essay.

"Robert Cormier Bibliography." *Fantastic Fiction*. Last accessed 24 Nov. 2003. http://www.fantasticfiction.co.uk/authors/Robert_Cormier.htm.
Lists Cormier's major works.

Biographies and Criticism

Gonsior, Marian C. "Robert Cormier." *Authors and Artists for Young Adults* 19: 75–85.
Biographical sketch with portrait, discussion of major works.

Nodelman, Perry. "Robert Cormier." Estes, *American Writers for Children Since 1960: Fiction* (*Dictionary of Literary Biography* 52): 214–27.
Discussion of literary career and influence.

"Robert (Edmund) Cormier." *Children's Literature Review* 55: 1–40.
Biographical sketch, discussion of literary career, excerpts from reviews and commentary.

Sieruta, Peter D. "Cormier, Robert." Silvey, *The Essential Guide to Children's Books and Their Creators*. 102–4.
Biographical sketch.

Bibliographies

"Cormier, Robert." Hendrickson, *Children's Literature: A Guide to the Criticism*. 75–77.
Lists books and articles about Cormier and his works.

SHARON CREECH, 1945–

Web Sites

"BookWire's Meet the Author: Sharon Creech." *BookWire*. 1 Oct. 2001. Last accessed 24 Nov. 2003. http://www.bookwire.com/bookwire/MeettheAuthor/Interview_Sharon_Creech.htm.
Interview with Creech.

Sharon Creech. Last accessed 24 Nov. 2003. http://www.sharoncreech.com/.
Author web site. Includes biographical information.

"Sharon Creech Interview." *ACHUKA*. Jan. 1998. Last accessed 23 Dec. 2003. http://www.achuka.co.uk/interviews/creech.php.
Interview with Creech.

"Sharon Creech's Biography." *Scholastic*. Last accessed 24 Nov. 2003. http://www2.scholastic.com/teachers/authorsandbooks/authorstudies/authorhome.jhtml?authorID=2152&collateralID=6243&displayName=Biography.
Biographical sketch.

Biographies and Criticism

Rodgers, Hannah F. "Creech, Sharon." Silvey, *The Essential Guide to Children's Books and Their Creators*. 109–10.
Biographical sketch.

"Sharon Creech." *Authors and Artists for Young Adults* 52: 47–54.
Biographical sketch with portrait, discussion of major works.

"Sharon Creech." *Children's Literature Review* 89: 22–52.
Biographical sketch, discussion of literary career, excerpts from reviews and commentary.

CHRIS CRUTCHER, 1946–

Web Sites

"Author Chats: Chris Crutcher." *New York Public Library*. 2003. Last accessed 23 Dec. 2003. http://summerreading.nypl.org/read2002/chats/crutcher_txt.html.
Transcript of a 2002 live online chat with Crutcher.

"Author Profile: Chris Crutcher." *TeenReads.com*. 2003. Last accessed 23 Dec. 2003. http://www.teenreads.com/authors/au-crutcher-chris-2.asp.
Biographical profile.

Chris Crutcher. Last accessed 23 Dec. 2003. http://www.aboutcrutcher.com/.
Author's home page. Includes biographical material.

Wilde, Susie. "Interview with Chris Crutcher." *Once Upon a Lap*. 1998. Last accessed 23 Dec. 2003. http://wildes.home.mindspring.com/OUAL/int/crutcherchris.html.
Interview with Crutcher, originally published in *BookPage* in 1993.

Biographies and Criticism

"Chris Crutcher." *Children's Literature Review* 28: 98–108.
Biographical sketch, discussion of literary career, excerpts from reviews and commentary.

Goldsmith, Francisca. "Crutcher, Chris(topher)." Cullinan and Person, *The Continuum Encyclopedia of Children's Literature*. 211–12.

Senick, Gerard J. "Chris Crutcher." *Authors and Artists for Young Adults* 39: 31–42.
Biographical sketch with portrait, discussion of major works.

KAREN CUSHMAN, 1941–

Web Sites

"Author Spotlight: Karen Cushman." *Houghton Mifflen Education Place*. Last accessed 24 Nov. 2003. http://www.eduplace.com/author/cushman/.
Biographical sketch; interview.

"Conversations: Making History into Fiction with Karen Cushman." *Writes of Passage*. 1996. Last accessed 24 Nov. 2003. http://www.writes.org/conversations/conver_6.html.
Interview with Cushman.

"Karen Cushman." *Kidspace @ The Internet Public Library*. 1999. Last accessed 24 Nov. 2003. http://www.ipl.org/div/kidspace/askauthor/cushmanbio.html. Short biographical article with portrait.

Ruddy, Tom, and Laurie Ferrone, with Kay E. Vandergrift. "Learning About Karen Cushman." *Vandergrift's Children's Literature Page*. 17 Mar. 1996. Last accessed 24 Nov. 2003. http://www.scils.rutgers.edu/~kvander/cushman.html.
Biographical sketch; discussion of major works.

Biographies and Criticism

Cuthbertson, Ken. "Karen Cushman." *Authors and Artists for Young Adults* 22: 37–43.
Biographical sketch with portrait, discussion of major works.

Horton, Nancy. "Cushman, Karen." Cullinan and Person, *The Continuum Encyclopedia of Children's Literature*. 21–25.
Biographical sketch.

"Karen Cushman." *Children's Literature Review* 55: 55–75.
Biographical sketch, discussion of literary career, excerpts from reviews and commentary.

ROALD DAHL, 1916–1990

Web Sites

"Audio Interviews: Roald Dahl." *BBC*. http://www.bbc.co.uk/bbcfour/audio interviews/profilepages/dahlr1.shtml.
Audio clips from 1988 BBC Four interview; brief biographical sketch.

Howard, Kristine. *Roald Dahl Fans.com*. 2003. Last accessed 24 Nov. 2003. http://www.roalddahlfans.com/index.php.
Includes a biographical sketch and information about Dahl's major works.

Liukkonen, Petri. "Roald Dahl." *Author's Calendar*. Ed. Ari Pesonen. 2000. Last accessed 24 Nov. 2003. http://www.kirjasto.sci.fi/rdahl.htm.
Biographical sketch and discussion of Dahl's major works.

"Roald Dahl." *BBC Books*. Last accessed 24 Nov. 2003. http://www.bbc.co.uk/arts/books/author/dahl/.
Portrait, biographical sketch, discussion of works.

"Roald Dahl Bibliography." *Fantastic Fiction*. Last accessed 24 Nov. 2003. http://www.fantasticfiction.co.uk/authors/Roald_Dahl.htm.
Lists Dahl's major works.

RoaldDahl.com. Last accessed 24 Nov. 2003. http://www.roalddahl.com.
Official web site with extensive resources pertaining to Dahl and his works.

Royer, Sharon E. "Roald Dahl and Sociology 101." *ALAN Review* 26: 1 (Fall 1998). Last accessed 24 Nov. 2003. http://scholar.lib.vt.edu/ejournals/ALAN/fall98/royer.html.
Critical essay.

Biographies and Criticism

Dahl, Roald. *Boy: Tales of Childhood*. New York: Farrar, Straus, Giroux, 1984.
Autobiography (covers Dahl's childhood).

———. *Going Solo*. New York: Farrar, Straus, Giroux, 1986.
Autobiography (covers Dahl's experiences in World War II).

"Dahl, Roald." *Something About the Author* 73: 39–46.
Biographical sketch with portrait, discussion of major works.

Horton, Nancy. "Dahl, Roald." Cullinan and Person, *The Continuum Encyclopedia of Children's Literature*. 216–17.
Biographical sketch.

"Roald Dahl." *Children's Literature Review* 41: 1–50.
Biographical sketch, discussion of literary career, excerpts from reviews and commentary.

Bibliographies

"Dahl, Roald." Hendrickson, *Children's Literature: A Guide to the Criticism*. 81–82.
Lists books and articles about Dahl.

PAULA DANZIGER, 1944–2004

Web Sites

"Author Profile: Paula Danziger." *Teenreads.com*. 2003. Last accessed 24 Nov. 2003. http://www.teenreads.com/authors/au-danziger-paula.asp.
Biographical profile and interview.

"Meet Paula Danziger." *Scholastic*. Last accessed 24 Nov. 2003. http://www.scholastic.com/titles/paula/.
Biographical sketch. Includes an audio file from Danziger.

"Paula Danziger." *Educational Paperbacks*. Last accessed 24 Nov. 2003. http://www.edupaperback.org/showauth.cfm?authid=25.
Biographical sketch and discussion of works.

"Paula Danziger." *Kidsread.com*. Last accessed 24 Nov. 2003. http://www.kidsreads.com/authors/au-danziger-paula.asp.
Photo, short biographical sketch, interview.

"Paula Danziger: She Just Gets Younger." *BookPage*. Last accessed 24 Nov. 2003. http://www.bookpage.com/0107bp/paula_danziger.html.
Portrait; interview with Danziger.

Biographies and Criticism

Jones, J. Sydney. "Danziger, Paula." *Something About the Author* 102: 56–62.
Biographical sketch with portrait, discussion of major works.

"Paula Danziger." *Children's Literature Review* 20: 49–56.
Biographical sketch, discussion of literary career, excerpts from reviews and commentary.

Phinney, Margaret Yatsevitch. "Danziger, Paula." Cullinan and Person, *The Continuum Encyclopedia of Children's Literature.* 218–19.
Biographical sketch.

MARGUERITE DE ANGELI, 1889–1987

Web Sites

"Marguerite deAngeli Collection." *Lapeer District Library, MI.* 2002. Last accessed 24 Nov. 2003. http://www.deangeli.lapeer.org/.
Guide to collection's archival holdings (much of which is online); biographical sketch and information about de Angeli's works.

Biographies and Criticism

Anderson, William. "de Angeli, Marguerite Lofft." Silvey, *Children's Books and Their Creators.* 190–91.
Biographical sketch.

"de Angeli, Marguerite." *Children's Literature Review* 1: 52–54.
Brief biographical sketch; excerpts from reviews and commentary.

"de Angeli, Marguerite (Lofft)." *Something About the Author* 100: 74–77.
Biographical sketch with portrait, discussion of major works.

Usrey, Malcolm. "Marguerite de Angeli." Cech, *American Writers for Children, 1900–1960* (*Dictionary of Literary Biography* 22): 110–24.
Discussion of literary career and influence.

JEAN DE BRUNHOFF, 1899–1937, AND LAURENT DE BRUNHOFF, 1925–

Web Sites

Babar. Last accessed 15 Nov. 2003. http://v1.nelvana.com/babar/.
Official web site. Includes music, graphics, biographical sketchs of Jean and Laurent de Brunhoff.

McAlister, Jamie. "Laurent de Brunhoff Still Reigns Over His Royal Legacy." *BookPage.* 2000. Last accessed 15 Nov. 2003. http://www.bookpage.com/0009bp/laurent_de_brunhoff.html.
Interview with Laurent de Brunhoff.

Biographies and Criticism

"de Brunhoff, Jean." *Something About the Author* 24: 56–59.
Biographical sketch with portrait, discussion of major works.

"de Brunhoff, Laurent." *Something About the Author* 24: 59–62.
Biographical sketch with portrait, discussion of major works.

"Jean de Brunhoff, Laurent de Brunhoff." *Children's Literature Review* 4: 19–40.
Biographical sketch, discussion of the Brunhoffs' literary careers, excerpts from reviews and commentary.

Rayburn, Shane. "de Brunhoff, Jean and Laurent." Cullinan and Person, *The Continuum Encyclopedia of Children's Literature*. 223–24.
Biographical sketch.

Weber, Nicholas Fox. *The Art of Babar: The Work of Jean and Laurent de Brunhoff*. New York: Harry N. Abrams.
Book-length study of the Babar books.

DANIEL DEFOE, 1660–1731

Web Sites

"Daniel Defoe." *CORAL (Caribbean Online Resource and Archive)*. 2002. Last accessed 22 Dec. 2003. http://www.caribbeanedu.com/coral/refcen/Biography/readbio.asp?id=59.
Biographical sketch.

Liukkonen, Petri. "Daniel Defoe." *Author's Calendar*. Ed. Ari Pesonen. 2000. Last accessed 24 Nov. 2003. http://www.kirjasto.sci.fi/defoe.htm.
Biographical sketch and discussion of Defoe's major works.

Project Gutenberg. 25 Dec. 2003. Last accessed 27 Dec. 2003. http://www.gutenberg.net/index.shtml.
Includes uncopyrighted online texts for several of Defoe's works, including *Robinson Crusoe* (use the "Find an Ebook" link to find texts by Defoe).

Biographies and Criticism

"Daniel Defoe." *Children's Literature Review* 61: 57–102.
Biographical sketch, discussion of literary career, excerpts from reviews and commentary.

Jones, J. Sydney. "Daniel Defoe." *Authors and Artists for Young Adults* 27: 49–61.
Biographical sketch with portrait, discussion of major works.

Novak, Maximillian E. "Daniel Defoe." Battestin, *British Novelists, 1660–1800, Part 1: A–L (Dictionary of Literary Biography* 39): 143–66.
Discussion of literary career and influence.

Person, Diane G. "Defoe, Daniel." Cullinan and Person, *The Continuum Encyclopedia of Children's Literature*. 225.
Biographical sketch.

TOMIE DePAOLA, 1934–

Web Sites

Tomie dePaola. Last accessed 10 Dec. 2003. http://www.tomiedepaola.com/.
Author web site. Includes biographical material.

"Tomie dePaola." *Kidsread.com*. 2000. Last accessed 10 Dec. 2003. http://www
.kidsreads.com/authors/au-depaola-tomie.asp.
Biographical sketch.

"Tomie dePaola." *Penguin Group (USA)*. 2000. Last accessed 10 Dec. 2003. http://
www.penguinputnam.com/Author/AuthorFrame?0000031532.
Biographical sketch on publisher web site.

Biographies and Criticism

Elleman, Barbara. "dePaola, Tomie." Cullinan and Person, *The Continuum Encyclopedia of Children's Literature*. 230–31.
Biographical sketch.

Senick, Gerard J. "dePaola, Tomie." *Something About the Author* 108: 59–72.
Biographical sketch with portrait, discussion of major works, primary and
secondary bibliographies.

Stoddard, Jewell. "dePaola, Tomie." Silvey, *The Essential Guide to Children's Books and Their Creators*. 121–22.
Biographical sketch.

CHARLES DICKENS, 1812–1870

Web Sites

"Charles Dickens." *The Victorian Web*. Last accessed 24 Nov. 2003. http://www
.victorianweb.org/authors/dickens/dickensov.html.
Biographical and scholarly information on Dickens.

"Charles Dickens Bibliography." *Fantastic Fiction*. Last accessed 24 Nov. 2003.
http://www.fantasticfiction.co.uk/authors/Charles_Dickens.htm.
List of Dickens's major works.

"The Dickens Project." *University of California*. Last accessed 24 Nov. 2003.
http://humwww.ucsc.edu/dickens/index.html.
An extensive site with biographical and scholarly resources.

Liukkonen, Petri. "Charles Dickens." *Author's Calendar*. Ed. Ari Pesonen. 2000. Last accessed 24 Nov. 2003. http://www.kirjasto.sci.fi/dickens.htm. Biographical sketch and discussion of Dickens's major works.

Project Gutenberg. 25 Dec. 2003. Last accessed 27 Dec. 2003. http://www.gutenberg .net/index.shtml. Includes uncopyrighted online texts for several of Dickens's works, including *A Christmas Carol* and *A Child's History of England* (use the "Find an Ebook" link to find texts by Dickens).

Biographies and Criticism

Ford, George H. "Charles Dickens." Nabel, Ira B., and William E. Fredeman, eds. *Victorian Novelists Before 1885* (*Dictionary of Literary Biography* 21): 89–124. Detroit, MI: Gale, 1983. Discussion of literary career and influence.

Jones, J. Sydney. "Charles Dickens." *Authors and Artists for Young Adults* 23: 47–61. Biographical sketch with portrait, discussion of major works.

Russell, David. "Charles Dickens." Cullinan and Person, *The Continuum Encyclopedia of Children's Literature*. 235. Biographical sketch.

Dictionaries, Encyclopedias, and Handbooks

Schlicke, Paul, ed. *Oxford Reader's Companion to Dickens*. Oxford: Oxford University Press, 1999. Includes entries on various aspects of Dickens's life and literary career.

Bibliographies

"Dickens, Charles (John Huffam)." Lynn, *Fantasy Literature for Children and Young Adults*. 685–86. Lists Dickens's major works.

CHARLES LUTWIDGE DODGSON (LEWIS CARROLL), 1832–1898

Web Sites

Birenbaum, Joel. *The Lewis Carroll Home Page*. Last accessed 15 Nov. 2003. http://www.lewiscarroll.org/carroll.html. Discusses Lewis Carroll online resources and documents, as well as print resources.

"Lewis Carroll." *Academy of American Poets*. 19 July 2000. Last accessed 15 Nov. 2003. http://www.poets.org/poets/poets.cfm?45442B7C000C010C. Biographical sketch, selected bibliography, links to related sites.

"Lewis Carroll: An Overview." *The Victorian Web*. Last accessed 15 Nov. 2003. http://www.victorianweb.org/authors/carroll/carrollov.html.
Biographical information, discussion of major works, links to related web sites.

Liukkonen, Petri. "Lewis Carroll." *Author's Calendar*. Ed. Ari Pesonen. 2000. Last accessed 15 Nov. 2003. http://www.kirjasto.sci.fi/lcarroll.htm.
Biographical sketch and discussion of Carroll's major works.

Project Gutenberg. 25 Dec. 2003. Last accessed 27 Dec. 2003. http://www .gutenberg.net/index.shtml.
Includes online texts for several of Carroll's works, including *Alice's Adventures in Wonderland* and *The Hunting of the Snark* (use the "Find an Ebook" link to find texts by Carroll).

Biographies and Criticism

"Lewis Carroll." *Authors and Artists for Young Adults* 39: 7–16.
Biographical sketch with portrait, discussion of major works.

"Lewis Carroll." *Children's Literature Review* 18: 38–80.
Biographical sketch, discussion of literary career, excerpts from reviews and commentary.

"Lewis Carroll." *Nineteenth-Century Literature Criticism* 53: 37–155.
Discussion of literary career; extensive discussion on critical commentary regarding Carroll's Alice books.

Mathis, Janelle B. "Carroll, Lewis." Cullinan and Person, *The Continuum Encyclopedia of Children's Literature*. 151–52.

Smith, Karen Patricia. "Lewis Carroll (Charles Lutwidge Dodgson)." *British Children's Writers 1800–1880* (*Dictionary of Literary Biography* 163): 56–69.
Discussion of literary career and influence.

Stoffel, Stephanie Lovett. *Lewis Carroll in Wonderland: The Life and Times of Alice and Her Creator*. New York: H. N. Abrams, 1997.
Book-length study of Carroll's life and literary career.

Bibliographies

"Carroll, Lewis (Charles Lutwidge Dodgson)." Hendrickson, *Children's Literature: A Guide to the Criticism*. 58–62.
Biographical sketch, discussion of Carroll's literary career. Includes excerpts from reviews and critical commentaries.

"Carroll, Lewis (pseud. of Charles Lutwidge Dodgson)." Lynn, *Fantasy Literature for Children and Young Adults*. 651–61.
Lists books and articles about Carroll and his works.

ARTHUR CONAN DOYLE, 1859–1930

Web Sites

Liukkonen, Petri. "Arthur Conan Doyle." *Author's Calendar*. Ed. Ari Pesonen. 2000. Last accessed 24 Nov. 2003. http://www.kirjasto.sci.fi/acdoyle.htm.
Biographical sketch and discussion of Doyle's major works.

The Official Web Site of the Sir Arthur Conan Doyle Literary Estate. 2000. Last accessed 24 Nov. 2003. http://www.sherlockholmesonline.org/.
Biographical sketch of Doyle and information about his works.

Project Gutenberg. 25 Dec. 2003. Last accessed 27 Dec. 2003. http://www .gutenberg.net/index.shtml.
Includes uncopyrighted online texts for several of Doyle's works, including *The Hound of the Baskervilles* and *The Adventures of Sherlock Holmes* (use the "Find an Ebook" link to find texts by Doyle).

Sherman, Michael. *221 BakerStreet.org*. 19 Feb. 2002. Last accessed 24 Nov. 2003. http://221bakerstreet.org/.
Extensive resources on Doyle and his Sherlock Holmes books.

"Sir Arthur Conan Doyle Bibliography." *Fantastic Fiction*. Last accessed 24 Nov. 2003. http://www.fantasticfiction.co.uk/authors/Sir_Arthur_Conan_Doyle .htm.
List of Doyle's major works.

Biographies and Criticism

Amster, Mara Ilyse. "Sherlock Holmes Books." Silvey, *Children's Books and Their Creators*. 599.
Short discussion of Sherlock Holmes series.

Cox, J. Randolph. "Sir Arthur Conan Doyle," Benstock, Bernard, and Thomas F. Staley, eds. *British Mystery Writers, 1860–1919* (*Dictionary of Literary Biography* 70): 112–34. Detroit, MI: Gale, 1988.
Discussion of literary career and influence.

Rampson, Nancy E. "Arthur Conan Doyle." *Authors and Artists for Young Adults* 14: 75–91.
Biographical sketch with portrait, discussion of major works.

Stashower, Daniel. *Teller of Tales: The Life of Arthur Conan Doyle*. New York: Holt, 1999.
Book-length study on Doyle and his literary career.

WILLIAM PÈNE DU BOIS, 1916–1993

Web Sites

"du Bois, William (Sherman) Pene." *CMS Library Information Center*. Last accessed 24 Nov. 2003. http://cms.westport.k12.ct.us/cmslmc/resources/authorstudy/authors/penedubois.htm.
Biographical sketch; discussion of works.

"William Pène du Bois." *Wikipedia*. 23 Oct. 2003. Last accessed 22 Dec. 2003. http://en2.wikipedia.org/wiki/William_P%e8ne_du_Bois.
Brief biographical sketch; discussion of major works.

Biographies and Criticism

"du Bois, William (Sherman) Pène." *Children's Literature Review* 1: 62–67.
Biographical sketch, discussion of literary career, excerpts from reviews and commentary.

Garness, Susan. "William Pène du Bois." Cech, *American Writers for Children, 1900–1960 (Dictionary of Literary Biography* 22): 27–37.
Discussion of literary career and influence.

Kasinec, Denise E. "Pène du Bois, William (Sherman)." *Something About the Author* 68: 178–82.
Biographical sketch with portrait, discussion of major works.

Small, Dede. "du Bois, William Pène." Cullinan and Person, *The Continuum Encyclopedia of Children's Literature*. 251–52.
Biographical sketch.

LOIS DUNCAN, 1934–

Web Sites

"Author Profile: Lois Duncan." *Teenreads.com*. 2003. Last accessed 24 Nov. 2003. http://www.teenreads.com/authors/au-duncan-lois.asp.
Biographical profile.

"Lois Duncan Bibliography." *Fantastic Fiction*. Last accessed 24 Nov. 2003. http://www.fantasticfiction.co.uk/authors/Lois_Duncan.htm.
Lists Duncan's major works.

Overstreet, Deborah Wilson. "Help! Help! An Analysis of Female Victims in the Novels of Lois Duncan." *ALAN Review* 21: 3 (Spring 1994). Last accessed 24 Nov. 2003. http://scholar.lib.vt.edu/ejournals/ALAN/spring94/Overstreet.html.
Critical essay.

Biographies and Criticism

Brennan, Carol. "Lois Duncan." *Authors and Artists for Young Adults* 34: 79–92.
Biographical sketch with portrait, discussion of major works.

Duncan, Lois. *Chapters: My Growth as a Writer*. Boston: Little, Brown, and Co.,
1982.
Autobiography.

"Lois Duncan (Steinmetz Arquette)." *Children's Literature Review* 29: 62–81.
Biographical sketch, discussion of literary career, excerpts from reviews
and commentary.

Small, Dede. "Duncan, Lois." Cullinan and Person, *The Continuum Encyclopedia
of Children's Literature*. 253–54.
Biographical sketch.

SYLVIA ENGDAHL, 1933–

Web Sites

Littlejohn, Carol. "Enchantress from the Stars: Sylvia Louise Engdahl, Star Trek
and Science Fiction." *ALAN Review* 25: 1 (Fall 1997). Last accessed 24
Nov. 2003. http://scholar.lib.vt.edu/ejournals/ALAN/fall97/littlejohn.html.
Critical essay.

Sylvia Engdahl. Last accessed 24 Nov. 2003. http://www.sylviaengdahl.com/.
Author's home page. Includes biographical information and links to related
sites.

"Sylvia Engdahl Interview." *sffworld.com*. Apr. 2001. Last accessed 24 Nov. 2003.
http://www.sffworld.com/authors/e/engdahl_sylvia/interviews/200104.html.
Interview.

Biographies and Criticism

"Autobiography Feature: Sylvia Louise Engdahl." *Something About the Author*
122: 35–54.
Autobiographical sketch.

Cuthbertson, Ken. "Sylvia Louise Engdahl." *Authors and Artists for Young Adults*
36: 59–65.
Biographical sketch with portrait, discussion of major works.

"Engdahl, Sylvia Louise." *Children's Literature Review* 2: 69–72.
Biographical sketch, discussion of literary career, excerpts from reviews
and commentary.

Sieruta, Peter D. "Engdahl, Sylvia." Silvey, *Children's Books and Their Creators*. 224–25.
Biographical sketch.

LOUISE ERDRICH, 1954–

Web Sites

"Louise Erdrich." *Kidsread.com*. Last accessed 24 Nov. 2003. http://www .kidsreads.com/authors/au-erdrich-louise.asp.
Biographical sketch and interview.

"Louise Erdrich, 1954–" *The Internet Public Library Native American Authors Project*. Last accessed 24 Nov. 2003. http://www.ipl.org/div/natam/bin/ browse.pl/A30.
Brief biographical sketch of Erdrich; links to online resources about her.

McNally, Amy Leigh, and Piyali Nath Dalal. "Louise Erdrich." *Voices from the Gaps: Women Writers of Color*. 27 May 1999. Last accessed 24 Nov. 2003. http://voices.cla.umn.edu/authors/ERDRICHlouise.html.
Biographical sketch, discussion of Erdrich's major works. Includes selected primary and secondary bibliographies.

Mudge, Alden. "Louise Erdrich Explores Mysteries and Miracles on the Reservation." *BookPage*. 2001. Last accessed 24 Nov. 2003. http://www.bookpage .com/0104bp/louise_erdrich.html.
Interview.

Nelson, Cary. "Louise Erdrich." *Modern American Poetry*. Last accessed 24 Nov. 2003. http://www.english.uiuc.edu/maps/poets/a_f/erdrich/erdrich.htm.
Includes a biographical sketch, discussion of various works, articles on Erdrich's works, and links to related web sites.

Reuben, Paul P. "Chapter 10: Late Twentieth Century—Louise Erdrich (1954–)." *PAL: Perspectives in American Literature—A Research and Reference Guide*. 11 Feb. 2003. Last accessed 24 Nov. 2003. http://www.csustan.edu/ english/reuben/pal/chap10/erdrich.html.
Includes primary and secondary bibliographies, portrait, links to related sites.

Spillman, Robert. "The Salon Interview: Louise Erdrich." www.salon.com. Last accessed 24 Nov. 2003. http://www.salon.com/weekly/interview960506 .html.
Interview.

Biographies and Criticism

Beidler, Peter G. "Louise Erdrich." Roemer, Kenneth M., ed. *Native American Writers of the United States* (*Dictionary of Literary Biography* 175): 84–100. Detroit, MI: Gale, 1997.
Biographical sketch, discussion of literary career.

Hafen, P. Jane. "Louise Erdrich." Cracroft, *Twentieth-Century American Western Writers, First Series* (*Dictionary of Literary Biography* 206): 85–96.
Biographical sketch, discussion of literary career.

"Louise Erdrich." *Authors and Artists for Young Adults* 47: 79–89.
Biographical sketch with portrait, discussion of major works.

Bibliographies

Beidler, Peter G., and Gay Barton. *Reader's Guide to the Novels of Louise Erdrich*. Columbia: University of Missouri Press, 1999.
Book-length study of Erdrich's novels.

WALTER FARLEY, 1915–1989

Web Sites

Walter Farley's "The Black Stallion." Last accessed 24 Nov. 2003. http://www.theblackstallion.com/main.html.
Official web site. Includes biographical information about Farley.

Biographies and Criticism

"Farley, Walter (Lorimer)." *Something About the Author* 132: 67–76.
Biographical sketch with portrait, discussion of major works.

Hurd, Elizabeth. "Walter Farley." Silvey, *The Essential Guide to Children's Books and Their Creators*. 151–52.
Biographical sketch.

Sadler, Philip A. "Walter Farley." Cech, *American Writers for Children, 1900–1960* (*Dictionary of Literary Biography* 22): 162–69.
Discussion of literary career and influence.

LOUISE FITZHUGH, 1928–1974

Web Sites

"Louise Fitzhugh." *CORAL (Caribbean Online Resource and Archive)*. 2002. Last accessed 22 Dec. 2003. http://www.caribbeanedu.com/coral/refcen/Biography/readbio.asp?id=78.
Biographical sketch.

Purple Socks: A Louise Fitzhugh Tribute Site. Last accessed 24 Nov. 2003. http://www.purple-socks.com/.
Includes biography, information about Fitzhugh's works, contemporaries, and friends, and links to other biographical and critical material written about Fitzhugh.

Biographies and Criticism

Hillstrom, Laurie Collier. "Louise Fitzhugh." *Authors and Artists for Young Adults* 18: 91–96.
Biographical sketch with portrait, discussion of major works.

"Louise Fitzhugh." *Children's Literature Review* 72: 152–91.
Biographical sketch, discussion of literary career, excerpts from reviews and commentary.

Nodelman, Perry. "Louise Fitzhugh." Estes, *American Writers for Children Since 1960: Fiction* (*Dictionary of Literary Biography* 52): 133–42.
Discussion of literary career and influence.

Sieruta, Peter. "Fitzhugh, Louise." Silvey, *The Essential Guide to Children's Books and Their Creators.* 156–57.
Biographical sketch.

Wolf, Virginia L. *Louise Fitzhugh.* New York: Twayne Publishers, 1991.
Discusses Fitzhugh's life and works.

SID FLEISCHMAN, 1920–

Web Sites

"Author Spotlight: Sid Fleischman." *HarperCollins.* Last accessed 23 Dec. 2003.
http://www.teenreads.com/authors/au-crutcher-chris-2.asp.
Biographical sketch.

Sid Fleischman. Last accessed 24 Nov. 2003. http://www.sidfleischman.com/.
Author web site. Includes biographical information.

"Sid Fleischman." *Kidsreads.com.* Last accessed 24 Nov. 2003. http://www.kids
reads.com/authors/au-fleischman-sid.asp.
Biographical sketch.

Biographies and Criticism

"(Albert) Sid(ney) Fleischman." *Children's Literature Review* 15: 101–17.
Biographical sketch, discussion of literary career, excerpts from reviews and commentary.

"Fleischman, (Albert) Sid(ney)." *Something About the Author* 96: 94–100.
Biographical sketch with portrait, discussion of major works.

Russell, David L. "Fleischman, (Albert) Sid(ney)." Cullinan and Person, *The Continuum Encyclopedia of Children's Literature.* 287–88.
Biographical sketch.

PAULA FOX, 1923–

Web Sites

"Paula Fox." *Random House*. Last accessed 24 Nov. 2003. http://www.random house.com/teachers/authors/pfox.html.
Biographical sketch.

Biographies and Criticism

Jones, J. Sydney. "Paula Fox." *Authors and Artists for Young Adults* 37: 83–92.
Biographical sketch with portrait, discussion of major works.

Moss, Anita. "Paula Fox." Estes, *American Writers for Children Since 1960: Fiction* (*Dictionary of Literary Biography* 52): 143–56.
Discussion of literary career and influence.

"Paula Fox." *Children's Literature Review* 44: 50–79.
Biographical sketch, discussion of literary career, excerpts from reviews and commentary.

Sutherland, Zena. "Fox, Paula." Silvey, *The Essential Guide to Children's Books and Their Creators*. 162–64.
Biographical sketch.

Bibliographies

"Fox, Paula." Hendrickson, *Children's Literature: A Guide to the Criticism*. 102–3.
Biographical sketch.

ANNE FRANK, 1929–1945

Web Sites

Anne Frank House. Last accessed 24 Nov. 2003. http://www.annefrank.nl/ned/default2.html.
Official web site of the Anne Frank House in Amsterdam. Includes extensive biographical information on Frank.

Irwin-DeVitis, Linda, and Beth Benjamin. "Can Anne Be Like Margot and Still Be Anne? Adolescent Girls' Development and Anne Frank: *The Diary of a Young Girl*." *ALAN Review* 23: 1 (Fall 1995). Last accessed 24 Nov. 2003. http://scholar.lib.vt.edu/ejournals/ALAN/fall95/Irwin-DeVitis.html.
Critical essay.

Liukkonen, Petri. "Anne Frank." *Author's Calendar*. Ed. Ari Pesonen. 2000. Last accessed 24 Nov. 2003. http://www.kirjasto.sci.fi/annefrank.htm.
Biographical sketch and discussion of Frank's work.

Biographies and Criticism

Garcia-Johnson, Ronie-Richele. "Anne Frank." *Authors and Artists for Young Adults* 12: 31–41.
Biographical sketch with portrait, discussion of major works.

Müller, Melissa. *Anne Frank: The Biography*. Trans. Rita and Robert Kimber. New York: Metropolitan Books/Henry Holt, 1998.
Book-length study of Frank's life.

JEAN FRITZ, 1915–

Web Sites

"Featured Author: Jean Fritz." *Carol Hurst's Children's Literature Web Site.* 1999. Last accessed 24 Nov. 2003. http://www.carolhurst.com/ authors/jfritz.html.
Short biographical sketch, discussion of selected works by Fritz.

"Jean Fritz." *Kidsreads.com.* 24 Nov. 2003. http://www.kidsreads.com/authors/ au-fritz-jean.asp.
Short biographical sketch.

"Meet the Author: Jean Fritz." *Children's Book Council.* 2002. Last accessed 27 Dec. 2003. http://www.cbcbooks.org/html/jeanfritz.html.
Biographical sketch.

Biographies and Criticism

"Autobiography Feature: Jean Fritz." *Something About the Author* 122: 74–85.
Autobiographical sketch.

Busbin, O. Mell. "Jean Fritz." Estes, *American Writers for Children Since 1960: Fiction (Dictionary of Literary Biography* 52): 156–67.
Discussion of literary career and influence.

"Fritz, Jean (Guttery)." *Something About the Author* 119: 54–58.
Biographical sketch; discussion of major works.

Horton, Nancy. "Fritz, Jean." Cullinan and Person, *The Continuum Encyclopedia of Children's Literature.* 300–301.

"Jean (Guttery) Fritz." *Children's Literature Review* 14: 102–23.
Biographical sketch, discussion of literary career, excerpts from reviews and commentary.

WANDA GÁG, 1893–1946

Web Sites

"Minnesota Authors Project Biographies: Wanda Gag." *Minnesota Historical Society.* 2002. Last accessed 24 Nov. 2003. http://people.mnhs.org/authors/ biog_detail.cfm?PersonID=Gag173.

Biographical sketch with a list of selected works, links to related web sites, and a secondary bibliography.

Ortakales, Denise. "Wanda Gág." *Women Children's Book Illustrators*. 24 Aug. 2002. Last accessed 24 Nov. 2003. http://www.ortakales.com/illustrators/. Biographical piece with portraits.

"Wanda Gag Papers." *de Grummond Collection*. 13 Dec. 1991. Last accessed 24 Nov. 2003. http://www.lib.usm.edu/%7Edegrum/html/research/findaids/gag .htm. Description of Wanda Gág archival papers held at the de Grummond Collection. Includes biographical sketch, discussion of major works.

Biographies and Criticism

"Gág, Wanda." *Something About the Author* 100: 100–104. Biographical sketch with portrait, discussion of major works.

Hearn, Michael Patrick. "Wanda Gág." Cech, American *Writers for Children, 1900–1960* (*Dictionary of Literary Biography* 22): 179–91. Discussion of literary career and influence.

James, J. Alison. "Gág, Wanda." Silvey, *The Essential Guide to Children's Books and Their Creators*. 169–71. Biographical sketch.

"Wanda Gág." *Children's Literature Review* 4: 78–94. Biographical sketch, discussion of literary career, excerpts from reviews and commentary.

Bibliographies

"Gág, Wanda." Hendrickson, *Children's Literature: A Guide to the Criticism*. 105–106. List of books and articles about Gág and her works.

"Wanda Gág." Rahn, *Children's Literature: An Annotated Bibliography of the History and Criticism*. 218–20. Lists books and articles on Gág.

NEIL GAIMAN, 1960–

Web Sites

Mitts-Smith, Debra. "Rising Star: Neil Gaiman." *Bulletin of the Centre for Children's Books*. 1 Oct. 2003. Last accessed 24 Nov. 2003. http://alexia .lis.uiuc.edu/puboff/bccb/1003focus.html. Discusses his children's works; mentions works of interest to young adults.

Neil Gaiman. Last accessed 24 Nov. 2003. http://www.neilgaiman.com/. Author web site. Includes biographical information.

Biographies and Criticism

Jones, J. Sydney. "Neil Gaiman." *Authors and Artists for Young Adults* 42: 69–79.
Biographical sketch with portrait, discussion of major works.

Sanders, Joe. "Neil Gaiman." Harris-Fain, *British Fantasy and Science-Fiction Writers Since 1960* (*Dictionary of Literary Biography* 261): 196–204.
Discussion of literary career and influence.

THEODOR SEUSS GEISEL
(DR. SEUSS), 1904–1991

Web Sites

"Dr. Seuss." *BBC Books*. Last accessed 12 Dec. 2003. http://www.bbc.co.uk/arts/books/author/seuss/.
Biographical sketch, discussion of major works, links to other sites of interest.

Dr. Seuss National Memorial at the Quadrangle. 2003. Last accessed 12 Dec. 2003. http://www.catinthehat.org/.
Includes biographical information.

"Happy Birthday, Dr. Seuss! The Read Across America Celebration." *Kidsread .com*. 2003. Last accessed 12 Dec. 2003. http://www.kidsreads.com/features/010221-seuss/seuss.asp.
Includes information about Seuss's life, books.

Seussville. 2003. Last accessed 12 Dec. 2003. http://www.seussville.com/seuss ville/.
Official web site. Includes biographical information.

Biographies and Criticism

"Dr. Seuss." *Children's Literature Review* 53: 119–45.
Biographical sketch, discussion of literary career, excerpts from reviews and commentary.

Fensch, Thomas, ed. *Of Sneetches and Whos and the Good Dr. Seuss: Essays on the Writings and Life of Theodor Geisel*. Jefferson, NC: McFarland & Co., 1997.
Critical essays on Seuss's works and literary career.

"Geisel, Theodor Seuss." *Something About the Author* 100: 104–9.
Biographical sketch with portrait, discussion of major works.

Kibler, Myra. "Theodor Seuss Geisel." Estes, *American Writers for Children Since 1960: Poets, Illustrators, and Nonfiction Authors* (*Dictionary of Literary Biography* 61). 75–86.
Discussion of literary career and influence.

Wilson, Nance. "Seuss, Dr. (Theodor Seuss Geisel)." Cullinan and Person, *The Continuum Encyclopedia of Children's Literature*. 709–11.
Biographical sketch.

Bibliographies

"Seuss, Dr. [Theodor Seuss Geisel]." Hendrickson, *Children's Literature: A Guide to the Criticism*. 244–46.
Lists books and articles about Seuss and his works.

JEAN CRAIGHEAD GEORGE, 1919–

Web Sites

"Author Profile: Jean Craighead George." *Teenreads.com*. Last accessed 24 Nov. 2003. http://www.teenreads.com/authors/au-george-jean.asp.
Biographical profile.

"George, Jean Craighead." *Educational Paperback Association*. Last accessed 24 Nov. 2003. http://www.edupaperback.org/showauth.cfm?authid=25.
Biographical profile.

George, Jean Craighead. "Words for the Young Child." *Cooperative Children's Book Center, School of Education, University of Wisconsin-Madison*. Last accessed 23 Dec. 2003. http://media.education.wisc.edu:8080/ramgen/ccbc/cz2000.rm.
Online video of the 2000 Charlotte Zolotow Lecture, given by Jean Craighead George.

Jean Craighead George. 2003. Last accessed 24 Nov. 2003. http://www.jean craigheadgeorge.com/.
Author web site. Includes biographical information.

"Jean Craighead George." *Kidsreads.com*. Last accessed 24 Nov. 2003. http://www.kidsreads.com/authors/au-george-jean-craighead.asp.
Portrait, short biographical profile, interview.

Biographies and Criticism

Chatton, Barbara A. "George, Jean Craighead." Silvey, *The Essential Guide to Children's Books and Their Creators*. 176–77.
Biographical sketch.

Hoyle, Karen Nelson. "Jean Craighead George." Estes, *American Writers for Children Since 1960: Fiction* (*Dictionary of Literary Biography* 52): 168–74.
Discussion of literary career and influence.

Vedder, Polly A. "Jean Craighead George." *Authors and Artists for Young Adults* 8: 61–72.
Biographical sketch with portrait, discussion of major works.

FRED GIPSON, 1908–1973

Web Sites

"Fred Gipson, 1908– . Papers, 1920–1973." *Harry Ransom Humanities Research Center at the University of Texas at Austin.* 17 Oct. 1996. Last accessed 30 Nov. 2003. http://www.hrc.utexas.edu/research/fa/gipson.hp .html.
Description of Fred Gipson archival materials at the Harry Ransom Humanities Research Center. Includes biographical information.

Biographies and Criticism

Cerra, Kathie Krieger. "Gipson, Fred (Frederick Benjamin Gipson)." Cullinan and Person, *The Continuum Encyclopedia of Children's Literature.* 320. Biographical sketch.

"Gipson, Frederick B. 1908– ." *Something About the Author* 2: 118–19. Biographical sketch with portrait, discussion of major works.

EDWARD GOREY, 1925–2000

Web Sites

Benfer, Amy. "People: Edward Gorey." *salon.com.* 2003. Last accessed 30 Nov. 2003. http://dir.salon.com/people/bc/2000/02/15/gorey/index.html?CP= SAL&DN=110.
Biographical sketch.

The Edward Gorey Bibliography Web Site. 7 Nov. 2003. Last accessed 30 Nov. 2003. http://www.fearofdolls.com/gorey.html.
Includes links to various online resources on Gorey as well as a list of his works.

Mudge, Alden. "Only Edward Gorey Could Turn Classic Dickens into 'The Haunted Tea-Cosy.' " *BookPage.* http://www.bookpage.com/9811bp/ edward_gorey.html.
Interview with Gorey.

"The West Wing: The Words of Edward Gorey." *Goreyography.* 2003. Last accessed 30 Nov. 2003. http://www.goreyography.com/west/west.htm.
Includes a biographical sketch, lists of works, links to related web sites.

Biographies and Criticism

"Edward Gorey." *Children's Literature Review* 36: 48–105.
Biographical sketch, discussion of literary career, excerpts from reviews and commentary.

Edwards, Eden K. "Gorey, Edward." Silvey, *The Essential Guide to Children's Books and Their Creators*. 179–80.
Biographical sketch.

Shelton, Pamela L. "Gorey, Edward." *Something About the Author* 70: 78–85.
Biographical sketch with portrait, discussion of major works.

Street, Douglas. "Edward Gorey." Estes, *American Writers for Children Since 1960: Poets, Illustrators, and Nonfiction Authors* (*Dictionary of Literary Biography* 52): 99–107.
Discussion of literary career and influence.

KENNETH GRAHAME, 1859–1932

Web Sites

Arthur, Rhona. "Kenneth Grahame: Essayist and Children's Writer, 1859–1932." 1 July 2000. *Scottish Authors*. Last accessed 30 Nov. 2003. http:// www .slainte.org.uk/Scotauth/grahadsw.htm.
Short biographical piece.

"Kenneth Grahame." *BBC Books*. Last accessed 11 Nov. 2003. http://www.bbc .co.uk/arts/books/author/grahame/.
Portrait, biographical sketch, list of important works.

"Kenneth Grahame Bibliography." *Fantastic Fiction*. Last accessed 30 Nov. 2003. http://www.fantasticfiction.co.uk/authors/Kenneth_Grahame.htm.
Lists Grahame's major works.

Project Gutenberg. 25 Dec. 2003. Last accessed 27 Dec. 2003. http://www .gutenberg.net/index.shtml.

Includes uncopyrighted online texts for several of Grahame's works, including *The Wind in the Willows* (use the "Find an Ebook" link to find texts by Grahame).

Biographies and Criticism

Dingley, R. J. "Kenneth Grahame." Zaidman, *British Children's Writers, 1880–1914* (*Dictionary of Literary Biography* 141): 87–102.
Discussion of literary career and influence.

"Grahame, Kenneth." *Something About the Author* 100: 109–13.
Biographical sketch with portrait, discussion of major works.

"Kenneth Grahame." *Children's Literature Review* 5: 109–36.
Biographical sketch, discussion of literary career, excerpts from reviews and commentary.

Russell, David L. "Grahame, Kenneth." Cullinan and Person, *The Continuum Encyclopedia of Children's Literature*. 328–29.
Biographical sketch.

Bibliographies

"Grahame, Kenneth." Hendrickson, *Children's Literature: A Guide to the Criticism*. 116–19.
    List of books and articles about Grahame and his works.

"Grahame, Kenneth." Lynn, *Fantasy Literature for Children and Young Adults*. 715–18.
    Lists books and articles about Grahame and his works.

KATE GREENAWAY, 1846–1901

Web Sites

"Kate Greenaway's Book of Games." *Children's Books Online*. Last accessed 30 Nov. 2003. http://www.childrensbooksonline.org/Greenaway_Games/index.htm.
    Online version of the Greenaway title (including her illustrations).

Ortakales, Denise. "Kate Greenaway (1846–1901)." *Women Children's Book Illustrators*. 24 Aug. 2002. Last accessed 30 Nov. 2003. http://www.ortakales.com/illustrators/.
    Biographical sketch; focuses on her illustration work.

Biographies and Criticism

"Greenaway, Kate." *Children's Literature Review* 6: 119–35.
    Biographical sketch, discussion of literary career, excerpts from reviews and commentary.

"Greenaway, Kate." *Something About the Author* 100: 113–16.
    Biographical sketch with portrait, discussion of major works.

Kiefer, Barbara. "Greenaway, Kate." Silvey, *The Essential Guide to Children's Books and Their Creators*. 182–84.
    Biographical sketch.

Lundin, Anne H. "Kate Greenaway." Zaidman, *British Children's Writers, 1880–1914* (*Dictionary of Literary Biography* 141): 103–17.
    Discussion of literary career and influence.

ELOISE GREENFIELD, 1929–

Web Sites

"Author Tracker: Eloise Greenfield." *HarperCollins*. Last accessed 23 Dec. 2003. http://www.harpercollins.com/catalog/author_xml.asp?AuthorId=12162.
    Biographical sketch from publisher web site.

Bishop, Rudine Sims. "Profile: Eloise Greenfield." *Language Arts* 74: 8 (Dec. 1997). Last accessed 23 Dec. 2003. http://www.ncte.org/library/files/Publications/Journals/la/0748-dec97/LA0748Eloise.PDF.
PDF file of *Language Arts* profile on Greenfield freely available online through the National Council of Teachers of English web site. Includes biographical information and a list of selected works by Greenfield.

"Eloise Greenfield's Biography." *Scholastic*. 2003. Last accessed 23 Dec. 2003. http://www2.scholastic.com/teachers/authorsandbooks/authorstudies/author home.jhtml?authorID=42&collateralID=5170.
Biographical sketch from publisher web site.

Wilde, Susie. "Interview with Eloise Greenfield." *Once Upon a Lap*. 1998. Last accessed 23 Dec. 2003. http://wildes.home.mindspring.com/OUAL/int/greenfieldeloise.html.
Interview with Greenfield, orginally published in 1993 in the *Independent*.

Biographies and Criticism

"Eloise Greenfield." *Children's Literature Review* 38: 76–96.
Biographical sketch, discussion of literary career, excerpts from reviews and commentary.

Horton, Nancy. "Greenfield, Eloise." Cullinan and Person, *The Continuum Encyclopedia of Children's Literature*. 332–33.
Biographical sketch.

Senick, Gerard J. "Greenfield, Eloise." *Something About the Author* 105: 85–93.
Biographical sketch, discussion of major works.

NIKKI GRIMES, 1950–

Web Sites

"Author Tracker: Nikki Grimes." *HarperCollins*. Last accessed 23 Dec. 2003. http://www.authortracker.com/author.asp?a=authorid&b=16749.
Biographical sketch.

Grimes, Nikki. "Riding (and Writing) on a Dare." *Booklinks* 9: 1 (Sept. 1999). http://www.ala.org/Content/ContentGroups/Book_Links1/Riding_and_Writing.htm.
An article by Grimes on how she approaches writing.

Nikki Grimes. 2003. Last accessed 23 Dec. 2003. http://nikkigrimes.com/.
Author's home page. Includes biographical information.

Biographies and Criticism

Chesner, Geralyn A. "Grimes, Nikki." Cullinan and Person, *The Continuum Encyclopedia of Children's Literature*. 336.
Biographical sketch.

"Grimes, Nikki." *Something About the Author* 136: 98–104.
Biographical sketch with portrait, discussion of major works.

"Nikki Grimes." *Authors and Artists for Young Adults* 53: 77–85.
Biographical sketch with portrait, discussion of major works.

"Nikki Grimes." *Children's Literature Review* 42: 88–95.
Biographical sketch, discussion of literary career, excerpts from reviews and commentary.

JACOB LUDWIG KARL GRIMM, 1785–1863, AND WILHELM KARL GRIMM, 1786–1859

Web Sites

Liukkonen, Petri. "Jacob Grimm." *Author's Calendar.* Ed. Ari Pesonen. 2000. Last accessed 30 Nov. 2003. http://www.kirjasto.sci.fi/jgrimm.htm.
Biographical sketch and discussion of Grimm's major works.

———. "Wilhelm Grimm." *Author's Calendar.* Ed. Ari Pesonen. 2000. Last accessed 30 Nov. 2003. http://www.kirjasto.sci.fi/wgrimm.htm.
Biographical sketch and discussion of Grimm's major works.

Project Gutenberg. 25 Dec. 2003. Last accessed 27 Dec. 2003. http://www.gutenberg.net/index.shtml.
Includes uncopyrighted online text of *Grimms' Fairy Tales* (use the "Find an Ebook" link to find it).

Vandergrift, Kay. "Snow White." *Vandergrift's Children's Literature Page.* Last accessed 30 Nov. 2003. http://scils.rutgers.edu/%7Ekvander/ snowwhite.html.
Includes background information, excerpts of literary criticism on *Snow White*, links to online full text of various versions, discussion of media treatment of *Snow White*, and extensive bibliography for further study.

Biographies and Criticism

Bottigheimer, Ruth B. "Jacob Grimm." Hardin, James, and Christoph E. Schweitzer, eds. *German Writers in the Age of Goethe, 1789–1832.* (*Dictionary of Literary Biography* 90): 100–107. Detroit, MI: Gale, 1989.
Discussion of literary career and influence.

———. "Wilhelm Grimm." Hardin and Schweitzer, *German Writers in the Age of Goethe, 1789–1832.* (*Dictionary of Literary Biography* 90). 108–13.
Discussion of literary career and influence.

"Grimm, Jacob Ludwig Karl, and Wilhelm Karl Grimm." *Something About the Author* 22: 126–51.
Biographical sketch with portrait, discussion of major works.

Russell, David L. "Grimm, Jacob, and Grimm, Wilhelm." Cullinan and Person, *The Continuum Encyclopedia of Children's Literature.* 336–38.
Biographical sketch.

JOHNNY GRUELLE, 1880–1938

Web Sites

"Author Tracker: Johnny Gruelle." *HarperCollins*. Last accessed 23 Dec. 2003.
   http://www.harpercollins.com/catalog/author_xml.asp?AuthorId=20113.
   Brief biographical sketch on publisher web site.

The Johnny Gruelle Raggedy Ann & Andy Museum. 2003. Last accessed 30 Nov.
   2003. http://www.raggedyann-museum.org/.
   Includes biographical information.

The Last Great Co.: The Home of Raggedy Ann and Andy. 7 Dec. 2003. Last ac-
   cessed 23 Dec. 2003. http://www.raggedyman.com/.
   Web site for a store operated by Kim Gruelle, a grandson of Johnny Gruelle.
The site includes information about Johnny Gruelle's life, and about Raggedy
Ann and Andy.

Biographies and Criticism

"Gruelle, John." *Something About the Author* 35: 106–9.
   Biographical sketch with portrait, discussion of major works.

VIRGINIA HAMILTON, 1936–2002

Web Sites

Daniels, Tyrone, Nicole Lesser, Tiffany McWhorter, and Cherie Zanders. "Virginia Hamilton." *Voices from the Gaps: Women Writers of Color*. 2003. Last
   accessed 30 Nov. 2003. http://voices.cla.umn.edu/authors/HAMILTON
   virginia.html.
   Biographical sketch, discussion of Hamilton's major works.

"Hamilton, Virginia." *Educational Paperback Association*. Last accessed 30 Nov.
   2003. http://www.edupaperback.org/showauth.cfm?authid=55.
   Biographical sketch.

Biographies and Criticism

Apseloff, Marilyn F. "Virginia Hamilton." Estes, *American Writers for Children
   Since 1960: Fiction* (*Dictionary of Literary Biography* 52): 174–84.
   Discussion of literary career and influence.

Shelton, Pamela L. "Virginia Hamilton." *Authors and Artists for Young Adults* 21:
   81–91.
   Biographical sketch with portrait, discussion of major works.

Sutherland, Zena. "Hamilton, Virginia." Silvey, *The Essential Guide to Children's
   Books and Their Creators*. 186–88.
   Biographical sketch.

"Virginia Hamilton." *Children's Literature Review* 40: 55–91.
Biographical sketch, discussion of literary career, excerpts from reviews and commentary.

Bibliographies

"Hamilton, Virginia." Hendrickson, *Children's Literature: A Guide to the Criticism.* 125–27.
Lists books and articles about the author and her works.

DANIEL HANDLER (LEMONY SNICKET), 1970–

Web Sites

"Lemony Snicket (Daniel Handler)." *Fantastic Fiction.* Last accessed 30 Nov. 2003. http://www.fantasticfiction.co.uk/authors/Lemony_Snicket.htm.
List of Lemony Snicket's major works.

A Series of Unfortunate Events. Last accessed 30 Nov. 2003. http://www.lemonysnicket.com.
Lemony Snicket's web site.

"A Series of Unfortunate Events by Lemony Snicket: Author Interview." Kidsreads.com. Last accessed 30 Nov. 2003. http://www.kidsreads.com/series/series-lemony-snicket-author.asp.
Biographical sketch, video short. Includes links to information about individual titles and characters.

Biographies and Criticism

"Lemony Snicket." *Authors and Artists for Young Adults* 46: 157–63.
Biographical sketch with portrait, discussion of major works.

"Lemony Snicket." *Children's Literature Review* 79: 184–207.
Biographical sketch, discussion of literary career, excerpts from reviews and commentary.

Person, Diane G. "Snicket, Lemony (Daniel Handler)." Cullinan and Person, *The Continuum Encyclopedia of Children's Literature.* 733–34.
Biographical sketch.

JOEL CHANDLER HARRIS (UNCLE REMUS), 1848–1908

Web Sites

Project Gutenberg. 25 Dec. 2003. Last accessed 27 Dec. 2003. http://www.gutenberg.net/index.shtml.
Includes uncopyrighted online texts for Harris's *Uncle Remus, His Songs and His Sayings* (use the "Find an Ebook" link to find texts by Harris).

Reuben, Paul P. "Chapter 5: Late Nineteenth Century—Joel Chandler Harris (1848–1908)." *PAL: Perspectives in American Literature—A Research and Reference Guide*. 3 Jan. 2003. Last accessed 30 Nov. 2003. http://www.csustan.edu/english/reuben/pal/chap5/harris.html.
Includes primary and secondary bibliographies, portrait, links to related sites.

"Uncle Remus." Ed. Melissa Murray and Dominic Perella. *University of Virginia*. http://xroads.virginia.edu/~UG97/remus/remus.html.
Includes biographical information, bibliography, some images and full text from Harris's works.

Biographies and Criticism

"Harris, Joel Chandler." *Something About the Author* 100: 117–22.
Biographical sketch with portrait, discussion of major works.

Keenan, Hugh T. "Joel Chandler Harris." Estes, *American Writers for Children Before 1900* (*Dictionary of Literary Biography* 42): 222–40.
Discussion of literary career and influence.

O'Laughlin, Michael. "Harris, Joel Chandler." Cullinan and Person, *The Continuum Encyclopedia of Children's Literature*. 348–49.
Biographical sketch.

Bibliographies

"Harris, Joel Chandler." Hendrickson, *Children's Literature: A Guide to the Criticism*. 129–30.
Lists books and articles about Harris and his works.

"Joel Chandler Harris." Rahn, *Children's Literature: An Annotated Bibliography of the History and Criticism*. 231–36.
Lists books and articles on Harris.

KEVIN HENKES, 1960–

Web Sites

Cary, Alice. "Special Interview with Author and Illustrator, Kevin Henkes." *BookPage*. 1996. Last accessed 30 Nov. 2003. http://www.bookpage.com/9609bp/childrens/lillyspurpleplasticpurse.html.
Interview; portrait.

Henkes, Kevin. "An Equivalent Happiness: Making It Out of Childhood." *Cooperative Children's Book Center, School of Education, University of Wisconsin-Madison*. Last accessed 23 Dec. 2003. http://media.education.wisc.edu:8080/ramgen/ccbc/cz2002.rm.
Online video of the 2002 Charlotte Zolotow Lecture, given by Kevin Henkes.

Kevin Henkes. 2003. http://www.kevinhenkes.com/. Last accessed 30 Nov. 2003.
Author's home page. Includes biographical information.

"Kevin Henkes." *Kidsread.com*. 2003. Last accessed 30 Nov. 2003. http://www
.kidsreads.com/authors/au-henkes-kevin.asp.
Biographical sketch.

Biographies and Criticism

"Kevin Henkes." *Children's Literature Review* 23: 124–31.
Biographical sketch, discussion of literary career, excerpts from reviews
and commentary.

Parravano, Martha V. "Kevin Henkes." Silvey, *The Essential Guide to Children's
Books and Their Creators*. 192–93.
Biographical sketch.

Telgen, Diane. "Henkes, Kevin." *Something About the Author* 108: 104–10.
Biographical sketch with portrait, discussion of major works.

S. E. HINTON, 1950–

Web Sites

"Audio Interview with S. E. Hinton." *Wired for Books*. Last accessed 30 Nov.
2003. http://wiredforbooks.org/sehinton/.
Audio file from 1987 interview with Hinton.

"Hinton, S. E." *Educational Paperback Association*. Last accessed 30 Nov. 2003.
http://www.edupaperback.org/showauth.cfm?authid=81.
Biographical sketch.

"S. E. Hinton." *Random House*. Last accessed 30 Nov. 2003. http://www.random
house.com/teachers/authors/sehi.html.
Portrait, biographical sketch.

S. E. Hinton.com. Last accessed 30 Nov. 2003. http://www.sehinton.com/.
Author web site. Includes biographical information.

"Susan Eloise Hinton." *CORAL (Caribbean Online Resource and Archive)*. 2002.
Last accessed 22 Dec. 2003. http://www.caribbeanedu.com/coral/refcen/
Biography/readbio.asp?id=110.
Biographical sketch.

Biographies and Criticism

Daly, Jay. *Presenting S. E. Hinton*. Boston: Twayne Publishers, 1987.
Critical commentary on Hinton's works.

Goldsmith, Francisca. "Hinton, S(usan) E(loise)." Cullinan and Person, *The Continuum Encyclopedia of Children's Literature*. 369–70.
Biographical sketch.

Jones, J. Sydney. "S. E. Hinton." *Authors and Artists for Young Adults* 33: 111–22.
Biographical sketch with portrait, discussion of major works.

"S(usan) E(loise) Hinton." *Children's Literature Review* 23: 132–50.
Biographical sketch, discussion of literary career, excerpts from reviews and commentary.

LILLIAN HOBAN, 1925–1998

Web Sites

"Russell and Lillian Hoban Papers." *de Grummond Collection.* 14 May 2002. Last accessed 30 Nov. 2003. http://www.lib.usm.edu/%7Edegrum/html/research/findaids/hobanrus.htm.
Description of Russell and Lillian Hoban archival papers at the de Grummond Collection. Includes biographical sketch, discussion of major works.

Biographies and Criticism

"Hoban, Lillian." *Something About the Author* 69: 106–109.
Biographical sketch with portrait, discussion of major works.

Knoth, Maeve Visser. "Hoban, Lillian." Silvey, *The Essential Guide to Children's Books and Their Creators.* 202.
Biographical sketch.

"Lillian Hoban." *Children's Literature Review* 67: 87–110.
Biographical sketch, discussion of literary career, excerpts from reviews and commentary.

RUSSELL HOBAN, 1925–

Web Sites

The Head of Orpheus: A Russell Hoban Reference Page. Ed. Dave Awl. 4 Nov. 2003. Last accessed 30 Nov. 2003. http://www.ocelotfactory.com/hoban/.
Biographical information, discussion of major works.

"Russell and Lillian Hoban Papers." *de Grummond Collection.* 14 May 2002. Last accessed 30 Nov. 2003. http://www.lib.usm.edu/%7Edegrum/html/research/findaids/hobanrus.htm.
Description of Russell and Lillian Hoban archival papers at the de Grummond Collection. Includes biographical sketch, discussion of major works.

Biographies and Criticism

Barrett, Mary Brigid. "Hoban, Russell." Silvey, *The Essential Guide to Children's Books and Their Creators.* 203–204.
Biographical sketch.

"Hoban, Russell." *Something About the Author* 136: 114–21.
Biographical sketch with portrait, discussion of major works.

"Russell Hoban." *Children's Literature Review* 69: 56–137.
    Biographical sketch, discussion of literary career, excerpts from reviews and commentary.

Wilkie-Stibbs, Christine. *Through the Narrow Gate: The Mythological Consciousness of Russell Hoban.* Rutherford, NJ: Fairleigh Dickinson University Press, 1989.
    Book-length study of Russell and his literary career.

Bibliographies

"Hoban, Russell." Hendrickson, *Children's Literature: A Guide to the Criticism.* 133–35.
    Lists books and articles about Russell and his works.

"Russell Hoban." Rahn, *Children's Literature: An Annotated Bibliography of the History and Criticism.* 243–45.
    Lists books and articles about Russell and his works.

TED HUGHES, 1930–1998

Web Sites

Earth Moon: A Ted Hughes Web Site. Ed. Claas Kazzer. Jan. 2003. Last accessed 30 Nov. 2003. http://www.earth-moon.org/.
    Includes biographical information and critical articles on Hughes's works.

"Ted Hughes." *Academy of American Poets.* 8 Feb. 2001. Last accessed 20 July 2001. http://www.poets.org/poets/poets.cfm?prmID=114.
    Biographical sketch, selected bibliography, links to related sites.

"Ted Hughes Bibliography." *Fantastic Fiction.* Last accessed 30 Nov. 2003. http://www.fantasticfiction.co.uk/authors/Ted_Hughes.htm.
    List of Hughes's primary works.

Biographies and Criticism

Hennessy, Michael. "Ted Hughes." Hunt, *British Children's Writers Since 1960* (*Dictionary of Literary Biography* 161): 197–209.
    Discussion of literary career and influence.

"Hughes, Ted." *Children's Literature Review* 3: 88–97.
    Biographical sketch, discussion of literary career, excerpts from reviews and commentary.

"Hughes, Ted." *Something About the Author* 49: 125–34.
    Biographical sketch with portrait, discussion of major works.

Rayburn, Shane. "Hughes, Ted." Cullinan and Person, *The Continuum Encyclopedia of Children's Literature.* 388–89.
    Biographical sketch.

BRIAN JACQUES, 1939–

Web Sites

"Brian Jacques." *Random House*. Last accessed 30 Nov. 2003. http://www
    .randomhouse.co.uk/redwall/.
    Includes a biographical sketch.

Lindsay, Dave. *Redwall Abbey*. 2003. Last accessed 30 Nov. 2003. http://www
    .redwall.org/.
    Author web site. Includes a biographical sketch and information about
Jacques's works.

"Meet the Writers: Brian Jacques." *Barnes and Noble*. 2003. Last accessed 23 Dec.
    2003.   http://www.barnesandnoble.com/writers/writer.asp?userid=0IAXS3
    ZLIT&cid=881720.
    Biographical sketch.

Wilde, Susie. "Interview with Brian Jacques." *Once Upon a Lap*. 1998. Last
    accessed 23 Dec. 2003. http://wildes.home.mindspring.com/OUAL/int/
    jacquesbrian.html.
    Interview with Jacques, originally published in *BookPage* in 1992.

Biographies and Criticism

"Brian Jacques." *Children's Literature Review* 21: 153–55.
    Excerpts from reviews and commentary.

"Jacques, Brian." *Something About the Author* 138: 141–47.
    Biographical sketch with portrait, discussion of major works.

Sieruta, Peter D. "Jacques, Brian." Silvey, *The Essential Guide to Children's
    Books and Their Creators*. 222–23.
    Biographical sketch.

RANDALL JARRELL, 1914–1965

Web Sites

Barr, Jason. "Faded Ink Spots (Randall Jarrell)." *Sabine Magazine*. Apr. 1998. Last
    accessed 30 Nov. 2003. http://www.sabine-mag.com/archive/ ar05010.htm.
    Biographical sketch.

Brunner, Edward, and Cary Nelson. "Randall Jarrell." *Modern American Poetry*.
    Last accessed 30 Nov. 2003. http://www.english.uiuc.edu/maps/poets/g_l/
    jarrell/jarrell.htm.
    Includes a biographical sketch, discussion of various works, articles on Jar-
rell's works, and links to related web sites.

"Randall Jarrell." *Academy of American Poets*. 7 Feb. 2001. Last accessed 30
    Nov. 2003. http://www.poets.org/poets/poets.cfm?prmID=9.
    Biographical sketch, selected bibliography, links to related sites.

Biographies and Criticism

Cech, John O. "Jarrell, Randall." Silvey, *The Essential Guide to Children's Books and Their Creators*. 225–26.
Biographical sketch.

"Jarrell, Randall." *Something About the Author* 7: 141–43.
Biographical sketch with portrait, discussion of major works.

Lovell, Barbara. "Randall Jarrell." Estes, *American Writers for Children Since 1960: Fiction* (*Dictionary of Literary Biography* 52): 209–13.
Discussion of literary career and influence. Includes a primary bibliography.

"Randall Jarrell." *Children's Literature Review* 6: 151–68.
Biographical sketch, discussion of literary career, excerpts from reviews and commentary.

Bibliographies

"Jarrell, Randall." Hendrickson, *Children's Literature: A Guide to the Criticism*. 144–46.
Lists books and articles about Jarrell and his works.

CROCKETT JOHNSON, 1906–1975

Web Sites

Nel, Philip. *The Crockett Johnson Home Page*. 16 Sept. 2003. Last accessed 30 Nov. 2003. http://www.ksu.edu/english/nelp/purple/.
Includes a biographical sketch, information about Johnson's works.

Biographies and Criticism

"Liesk, David (Johnson), 1906–1975, (Crockett Johnson)." *Something About the Author* 30: 141–44.
Biographical sketch with portrait, discussion of major works.

Saunders, Sheryl Lee. "Johnson, Crockett." Silvey, *The Essential Guide to Children's Books and Their Creators*. 229–30.
Biographical sketch.

WILLIAM JOYCE, 1957–

Web Sites

Cary, Alice. "Special Interview with Author and Illustrator, William Joyce." *BookPage*. 1996. Last accessed 5 Dec. 2003. http://www.bookpage.com/9610bp/childrens/theleafmen.html.
Portraits; interview.

"The World of William Joyce." *HarperChildrens.com.* 1998. Last accessed 5 Dec. 2003. http://www.harperchildrens.com/williamjoyce/homepage. htm.
Author's page at publisher web site. Includes biographical material.

Biographies and Criticism

Edwards, Eden K. "Joyce, William." Silvey, *The Essential Guide to Children's Books and Their Creators.* 231–32.
Biographical sketch.

"Joyce, William." *Something About the Author* 118: 92–96.
Biographical sketch, discussion of major works.

"William Joyce." *Children's Literature Review* 26: 83–86.
Biographical sketch, discussion of literary career, excerpts from reviews and commentary.

EZRA JACK KEATS, 1916–1983

Web Sites

"Author Tracker: Ezra Jack Keats." *HarperCollins.* Last accessed 27 Dec. 2003. http://www.harpercollins.com/catalog/author_xml.asp?AuthorId=12298.
Biographical sketch.

"Ezra Jack Keats." *Penguin Group (USA).* 2003. Last accessed 5 Dec. 2003. http://www.penguinputnam.com/Author/AuthorFrame?0000013750.
Biographical sketch from publisher web site.

"The Ezra Jack Keats Collection." *The de Grummond Children's Literature Collection.* 2 May 2002. Last accessed 5 Dec. 2003. http://www.lib.usm.edu/~degrum/html/collectionhl/Keats/ch-keats.
Description of Ezra Jack Keats archival papers at the de Grummond Collection. Includes a biographical sketch, virtual exhibit of his work, and primary bibliography.

The Official Ezra Jack Keats Website. Last accessed 5 Dec. 2003. http://www.ezra-jack-keats.org/.
Sponsored by the Ezra Jack Keats Foundation. Includes a biographical sketch and information about Keats's works.

Biographies and Criticism

Burns, Mary Mehlman. "Keats, Ezra Jack." Silvey, *The Essential Guide to Children's Books and Their Creators.* 234.
Biographical sketch.

"Ezra Jack Keats." *Children's Literature Review* 35: 82–143.
Biographical sketch, discussion of literary career, excerpts from reviews and commentary.

"Keats, Ezra Jack." *Something About the Author* 57: 77–87.
    Biographical sketch with portrait, discussion of major works.

Seiter, Richard. "Ezra Jack Keats." Estes, *American Writers for Children Since 1960: Poets, Illustrators, and Nonfiction Authors* (*Dictionary of Literary Biography* 61): 116–25.
    Discussion of literary career and influence.

M. E. KERR, 1927–

Web Sites

Danielson, Audrey Marie. "Author Profile: M. E. Kerr." *Teenreads.com.* 2003. Last accessed 5 Dec. 2003. http://www.teenreads.com/authors/au-kerr-me .asp.
    Biographical sketch.

Koh, Michelle. *The M. E. Kerr and Mary James Site.* 13 Nov 2003. Last accessed 5 Dec. 2003. http://www.mekerr.com/index1.html.
    Author's official web site. Includes biographical material and audio files from interviews with Kerr.

Biographies and Criticism

"Autobiography Feature: M. E. Kerr." *Something About the Author* 111: 97–111.
    Autobiographical sketch.

Day, Frances Ann. "M. E. Kerr." *Lesbian and Gay Voices: An Annotated Bibliography and Guide to Literature for Childen and Young Adults.* Westport, CT: Greenwood. 201–5.
    Includes a biographical profile of Kerr.

Kantar, Andrew. "Kerr, M. E. (Marijane Agnes Meaker)." Cullinan and Person, *The Continuum Encyclopedia of Children's Literature.* 437–38.
    Biographical sketch.

"M. E. Kerr." *Children's Literature Review* 29: 127–59.
    Biographical sketch, discussion of literary career, excerpts from reviews and commentary.

Rampson, Nancy. "M. E. Kerr." *Authors and Artists for Young Adults* 23: 87–96.
    Biographical sketch with portrait, discussion of major works.

Bibliographies

"Kerr, M. E. [Marijane Meaker]." Hendrickson, *Children's Literature: A Guide to the Criticism.* 151.
    Lists books and articles on Kerr and her works.

RUDYARD KIPLING, 1865–1936

Web Sites

The Kipling Society. Ed. John Radcliffe. Last accessed 5 Dec. 200 http://www
.kipling.org.uk/.
Site for the Kipling Society. Includes a biographical sketch of Kipling.

"Rudyard Kipling." *Academy of American Poets.* 2 July 2001. Last accessed 5
Dec. 2003. http://www.poets.org/poets/poets.cfm?prmID=137.
Biographical sketch, selected bibliography, links to related sites.

"Rudyard Kipling." *Fantastic Fiction.* 2003. Last accessed 5 Dec. 2003. http://
www.fantasticfiction.co.uk/authors/Rudyard_Kipling.htm.
Lists Kipling's major works.

Project Gutenberg. 25 Dec. 2003. Last accessed 27 Dec. 2003. http://www
.gutenberg.net/index.shtml.
   Includes uncopyrighted online texts for several of Kipling's works, including *The Jungle Book* (use the "Find an Ebook" link to find texts by Kipling).

Biographies and Criticism

"Kipling, (Joseph) Rudyard." *Something About the Author* 100: 133–41.
Biographical sketch with portrait, discussion of major works.

Mathis, Janelle B. "Kipling, Rudyard." Cullinan and Person, *The Continuum Encyclopedia of Children's Literature.* 443–44.
Biographical sketch.

McCuchan, Corinne. "Rudyard Kipling." Zaidman, *British Children's Writers,
1880–1914* (*Dictionary of Literary Biography* 141): 151–72.
Discussion of literary career and influence.

"Rudyard Kipling." *Children's Literature Review* 39: 74–118.
   Biographical sketch, discussion of literary career, excerpts from reviews
and commentary.

Bibliographies

"Kipling, Rudyard." Hendrickson, *Children's Literature: A Guide to the Criticism.* 152–56.
List of books and articles about Kipling and his works.

"Rudyard Kipling." Rahn, *Children's Literature: An Annotated Bibliography of
the History and Criticism.* 254–62.
Lists books and articles about Kipling and his works.

E. L. KONIGSBURG, 1930–

Web Sites

"E. L. Konigsburg." *Houghton Mifflin.* 2000. Last accessed 5 Dec. 2003. http://www.eduplace.com/kids/hmr/mtai/konigsburg.html.
Publisher web site. Includes a biographical sketch.

"E. L. Konigsburg." *Teachers @ Random (Random House Children's Books).* 2003. Last accessed 27 Dec. 2003. http://www.randomhouse.com/teachers/catalog/display_bio.pperl?isbn=0440400341.
Biographical sketch on publisher web site.

Biographies and Criticism

"E. L. Konigsburg." *Children's Literature Review* 81: 122–79.
Biographical sketch, discussion of literary career, excerpts from reviews and commentary.

Goldsmith, Francisca. "Konigsburg, E(laine) L(obl)." Cullinan and Person, *The Continuum Encyclopedia of Children's Literature.* 447–49.
Biographical sketch.

Hanks, Dorrel Thomas. *E. L. Konigsburg.* New York: Twayne Publishers, 1992.
Critical commentary on Konigsburg's works.

Jones, J. Sydney. "E. L. Konigsburg." *Authors and Artists for Young Adults* 41: 89–97.
Biographical sketch with portrait, discussion of major works.

Nodelman, Perry. "E. L. Konigsburg." Estes, *American Writers for Children Since 1960: Fiction (Dictionary of Literary Biography* 52). 214–27.
Discussion of literary career and influence.

Bibliographies

"Konigsburg, E(laine) L(obl)." Lynn, *Fantasy Literature for Children and Young Adults.* 753–54.
Lists books and articles about Konigsburg and her works.

CHARLES LAMB, 1775–1834, AND MARY ANN LAMB, 1764–1847

Web Sites

"Charles Lamb (1775–1834)." *Internet Public Library Online Literary Criticism Collection.* 12 June 2002. Last accessed 8 Dec. 2003. http://www.ipl.org/div/litcrit/bin/litcrit.out.pl?au=lam-561.
Links to pages that include literary criticism or biographical information about Charles Lamb.

"Mary Ann Lamb (1764–1847)." *Internet Public Library Online Literary Criticism Collection*. 12 June 2002. Last accessed 8 Dec. 2003. http://ipl.si .umich.edu/div/litcrit/bin/litcrit.out.pl?au=lam-734.

Links to pages that include literary criticism or biographical information about Mary Ann Lamb.

Project Gutenberg. 25 Dec. 2003. Last accessed 27 Dec. 2003. http://www .gutenberg.net/index.shtml.

Includes uncopyrighted online texts for several of the Lambs' works, including *Tales from Shakespeare* (use the "Find an Ebook" link to find texts by the Lambs).

Biographies and Criticism

"Lamb, Charles." *Something About the Author* 17: 101–12.
Biographical sketch with portrait, discussion of major works.

"Lamb, Mary." *Something About the Author* 17: 112–16.
Biographical sketch with portrait, discussion of major works.

Rayburn, Shane. "Lamb, Charles and Mary." Cullinan and Person, *The Continuum Encyclopedia of Children's Literature*. 457.
Biographical sketch.

White, Judy Anne. "Charles Lamb and Mary Lamb." Khorana, *British Children's Writers, 1800–1880* (*Dictionary of Literary Biography* 163): 159–66.
Discussion of literary career and influence.

ANDREW LANG, 1844–1912

Web Sites

"Andrew Lang Bibliography." *Fantastic Fiction*. 2003. Last accessed 8 Dec. 2003. http://www.fantasticfiction.co.uk/authors/Andrew_Lang.htm.
List of Lang's major works.

"The Electronic Text Center: Subject: Young Readers." *University of Virginia Library*. Last accessed 8 Dec. 2003. http://etext.lib.virginia.edu/subjects/ Young-Readers.html.
Includes the *Yellow, Red, Blue*, and *Violet Fairy* books.

Project Gutenberg. 25 Dec. 2003. Last accessed 27 Dec. 2003. http://www .gutenberg.net/index.shtml.
Includes uncopyrighted online texts for several of Lang's works, including *The Arabian Nights*, and many of the fairy-tale books (use the "Find an Ebook" link to find texts by Lang).

Stott, Louis. "Andrew Lang: Scholar and Man of Letters." *Scottish Authors*. 1 July 2000. Last accessed 8 Dec. 2003. http://www.slainte.org.uk/Scotauth/ langadsw.htm.
Biographical sketch.

Biographies and Criticism

Imdieke, Sandra. "Lang, Andrew." Cullinan and Person, *The Continuum Encyclopedia of Children's Literature*. 457–58.
Biographical sketch.

"Lang, Andrew." *Something About the Author* 16: 178–87.
Biographical sketch with portrait, discussion of major works.

Susina, Jan. "Andrew Lang." Zaidman, *British Children's Writers, 1880–1914* (*Dictionary of Literary Biography* 141): 173–85.
Discussion of literary career and influence.

Bibliographies

"Lang, Andrew." Lynn, *Fantasy Literature for Children and Young Adults*. 757.
List of books and articles about Lang and his works.

ROBERT LAWSON, 1892–1957

Web Sites

"Robert Lawson." *The Scoop*. Last accessed 8 Dec. 2003. http://www.friend
.ly.net/scoop/biographies/lawsonrobert/index.html.
Biographical sketch.

Biographies and Criticism

Horton, Nancy. "Lawson, Robert." Cullinan and Person, *The Continuum Encyclopedia of Children's Literature*. 467–68.
Biographical sketch.

Inman, Sue Lile. "Robert Lawson." Cech, *American Writers for Children, 1900–1960* (*Dictionary of Literary Biography* 22): 231–41.
Discussion of literary career and influence.

"Lawson, Robert." *Something About the Author* 100: 142–46.
Biographical sketch with portrait, discussion of major works.

"Robert Lawson." *Children's Literature Review* 73: 93–125.
Biographical sketch, discussion of literary career, excerpts from reviews and commentary.

Schmidt, Gary D. *Robert Lawson*. New York: Twayne Publishers, 1997.
Critical commentary on Lawson's works.

EDWARD LEAR, 1812–1888

Web Sites

"Edward Lear." *Academy of American Poets*. 13 June 2001. Last accessed 8 Dec. 2003. http://www.poets.org/poets/poets.cfm?prmID=141.
Biographical sketch, selected bibliography, links to related sites.

"Edward Lear." *CORAL (Caribbean Online Resource and Archive)*. 2002. Last accessed 22 Dec. 2003. http://www.caribbeanedu.com/coral/refcen/Biography/readbio.asp?id=131.
Biographical sketch.

"Edward Lear." *The Knitting Circle (South Bank University)*. 11 Sept. 2000. Last accessed Dec. 2003. http://myweb.lsbu.ac.uk/~stafflag/edwardlear.html.
Short biographical essay, list of Lear's major works.

Graziosi, Marco. *Edward Lear Home Page*. 22 Feb. 2003. Last accessed 8 Dec. 2003. http://www.nonsenselit.org/Lear/.
Includes biographical information and essays on Lear and his works.

Project Gutenberg. 25 Dec. 2003. Last accessed 27 Dec. 2003. http://www.gutenberg.net/index.shtml.
Includes uncopyrighted online texts for Lear's *The Book of Nonsense* (use the "Find an Ebook" link to find texts by Lear).

Biographies and Criticism

Anderson, Celia Catlett. "Edward Lear." Khorana, *British Children's Writers, 1800–1880 (Dictionary of Literary Biography* 163): 167–76.
Discussion of literary career and influence.

"Edward Lear." *Children's Literature Review* 75: 142–214.
Biographical sketch, discussion of literary career, excerpts from reviews and commentary.

"Lear, Edward." *Something About the Author* 100: 146–50.
Biographical sketch with portrait, discussion of major works.

Pilgrim, Jodi. "Lear, Edward." Cullinan and Person, *The Continuum Encyclopedia of Children's Literature*. 469–70.
Biographical Sketch.

Bibliographies

"Edward Lear." Rahn, *Children's Literature: An Annotated Bibliography of the History and Criticism*. 266–71.
Lists books and articles about Lear and his works.

"Lear, Edward." Hendrickson, *Children's Literature: A Guide to the Criticism*. 162–64.
Lists books and articles about Lear and his works.

URSULA K. LE GUIN, 1929–

Web Sites

"Author Profile: Ursula Le Guin." *Teenreads.com*. 2003. Last accessed 8 Dec. 2003. http://www.teenreads.com/authors/au-leguin-ursula.asp.
Biographical sketch.

Gevers, Nick. "Driven by a Different Chauffeur: An Interview with Ursula K. Le Guin." *SF Site*. Nov.–Dec. 2001. Last accessed 8 Dec. 2003. http://www.sfsite.com/03a/ul123.htm.
Interview with Le Guin.

Griffin, Jan M. "Ursula Le Guin's Magical World of Earthsea." *ALAN Review* 23: 3 (Spring 1996). Last accessed 8 Dec. 2003. http://scholar.lib.vt.edu/ejournals/ALAN/spring96/griffin.html.
Critical essay.

Le Guin's World. 11 Feb. 2003. Last accessed 8 Dec. 2003. http://hem1.passagen.se/peson42/lgw/.
Site devoted to Le Guin and her works.

Liukkonen, Petri. "Ursula K. Le Guin." *Author's Calendar*. Ed. Ari Pesonen. 2000. Last accessed 8 Dec. 2003. http://www.kirjasto.sci.fi/leguin.htm.
Biographical sketch and discussion of Le Guin's major works.

Ursula K. Le Guin. 2 Dec. 2003. Last accessed 8 Dec. 2003. http://www.ursulakleguin.com/.
Author web site. Includes biographical material.

Biographies and Criticism

Burgess, Susan A. "Le Guin, Ursula." Silvey, *The Essential Guide to Children's Books and Their Creators*. 255–57.
Gordon, Andrew. "Ursula K. Le Guin." Estes, *American Writers for Children Since 1960: Fiction* (*Dictionary of Literary Biography* 52): 233–41.
Discussion of literary career and influence.

Senick, Gerard J. "Ursula K. Le Guin." *Authors and Artists for Young Adults*: 27: 119–33.
Biographical sketch with portrait, discussion of major works.

"Ursula K(roeber) Le Guin." *Children's Literature Review* 28: 144–88.
Biographical sketch, discussion of literary career, excerpts from reviews and commentary.

Bibliographies

Cogell, Elizabeth Cummins. *Ursula K. LeGuin: A Primary and Secondary Bibliography*. Boston: G. K. Hall, 1983.
Book-length list of Le Guin's works, as well as books and articles about Le Guin and her works.

"Le Guin, Ursula K(roeber)." Lynn, *Fantasy Literature for Children and Young Adults*. 761–68.
   Lists books and articles about Le Guin and her works.

MADELEINE L'ENGLE, 1918–

Web Sites

"Author Profile: Madeleine L'Engle." *Teenreads.com*. 2003. Last accessed 5 Dec. 2003. http://www.teenreads.com/authors/au-lengle-madeleine.asp.
   Biographical sketch.

Madeleine L'Engle. 2001. Last accessed 5 Dec. 2003. http://www.madeleine lengle.com/.
   Author web site. Includes biographical information.

"Madeleine L'Engle." *CORAL (Caribbean Online Resource and Archive)*. 2002. Last accessed 22 Dec. 2003. http://www.caribbeanedu.com/coral/refcen/ Biography/readbio.asp?id=133.
   Biographical sketch.

"Madeleine L'Engle." *Fantastic Fiction*. 2003. Last accessed 5 Dec. 2003. http:// www.fantasticfiction.co.uk/authors/Madeleine_LEngle.htm.
   Lists L'Engle's major works.

"Madeleine L'Engle." *Kidsread.com*. 2003. Last accessed 5 Dec. 2003. http:// www.kidsreads.com/series/series-time-author.asp.
   Biographical sketch.

Biographies and Criticism

Cullinan, Bernice E. "L'Engle, Madeleine." Cullinan and Person, *The Continuum Encyclopedia of Children's Literature*. 472–73.
   Biographical sketch.

"L'Engle, Madeleine." *Something About the Author* 128: 148–54.
   Biographical sketch with portrait, discussion of major works.

"Madeleine (Camp Franklin) L'Engle." *Children's Literature Review* 57: 73–96.
   Biographical sketch, discussion of literary career, excerpts from reviews and commentary.

Parker, Marygail G. "Madeleine L'Engle." Estes, *American Writers for Children Since 1960: Fiction* (*Dictionary of Literary Biography* 52): 241–49.
   Discussion of literary career.

Bibliographies

"L'Engle, Madeleine." Lynn, *Fantasy Literature for Children and Young Adults*. 768–70.
   Lists books and articles about L'Engle and her works.

LOIS LENSKI, 1893–1974

Web Sites

"Lois Lenski Collection." *Walter Clinton Jackson Library*. 2 Sept. 2003. Last accessed 8 Dec. 2003. http://library.uncg.edu/depts/speccoll/lenski/.
Description of Lois Lenski archival papers at the Walter Clinton Jackson Library. Includes biographical sketch, discussion of major works.

Ortakales, Denise. "Lois Lenski." *Women Children's Illustrators*. 24 Aug. 2002. Last accessed 8 Dec. 2003. http://www.ortakales.com/illustrators/.
Biographical sketch.

Biographies and Criticism

Horton, Nancy. "Lenski, Lois." Cullinan and Person, *The Continuum Encyclopedia of Children's Literature*. 474–75.
Biographical sketch.

"Lenski, Lois." *Something About the Author* 100: 150–55.
Biographical sketch with portrait, discussion of major works.

"Lois Lenski." *Children's Literature Review* 26: 87–125.
Biographical sketch, discussion of literary career, excerpts from reviews and commentary.

Ranta, Taimi M. "Lois Lenski." Cech, *American Writers for Children, 1900–1960* (*Dictionary of Literary Biography* 22): 241–52.
Discussion of literary career and influence.

JULIUS LESTER, 1939–

Web Sites

"Julius Lester." *CORAL (Caribbean Online Resource and Archive)*. 2002. Last accessed 22 Dec. 2003. http://www.caribbeanedu.com/coral/refcen/Biography/readbio.asp?id=135.
Biographical sketch.

"Julius Lester." *Penguin Group (USA)*. 2000. Last accessed 9 Dec. 2003. http://www.penguinputnam.com/Author/AuthorFrame?0000015438.
Biographical sketch from publisher web site.

Lester, Julius. "Point of View: A Sacred Trust." *Cooperative Children's Book Center, School of Education, University of Wisconsin-Madison*. Last accessed 23 Dec. 2003. http://media.education.wisc.edu:8080/ramgen/ccbc/ibby1999four.rm.
Online video of a presentation by Julius Lester at the Third Biennial IBBY Regional Conference, in Madison, Wisconsin, from October 8–9, 1999 (Betsy Hearne, who appears first in the video, introduced him).

Biographies and Criticism

"Julius Lester." *Authors and Artists for Young Adults* 51: 137–46.
   Biographical sketch with portrait, discussion of major works.

"Julius Lester." *Children's Literature Review* 41: 91–115.
   Biographical sketch, discussion of literary career, excerpts from reviews and commentary.

Sieruta, Peter D. "Lester, Julius." Silvey, *The Essential Guide to Children's Books and Their Creators*. 260–61.
   Biographical sketch.

GAIL LEVINE, 1947–

Web Sites

"Gail Levine." *HarperChildrens.com.* Last accessed 8 Dec. 2003. http://www .harperchildrens.com/hch/author/author/levine/index.asp.
   Biographical sketch, interview.

"Gail Levine." *Kidsread.com.* 2003. Last accessed 8 Dec. 2003. http://www .kidsreads.com/authors/au-levine-gail-carson.asp.
   Biographical sketch.

"Interview with Children's Book Author Gail Carson Levine." *Cynthia Leitich Smith Children's Literature Resources.* Last accessed 8 Dec. 2003. http:// www.cynthialeitichsmith.com/auth-illGailCarsonLevine.htm.
   Interview with Levine.

Biographies and Criticism

"Gail Carson Levine." *Children's Literature Review* 85: 111–25.
   Biographical sketch, discussion of literary career, excerpts from reviews and commentary.

Jones, J. Sydney. "Gail Carson Levine." *Authors and Artists for Young Adults* 37: 129–35.
   Biographical sketch with portrait, discussion of major works.

Wroclawski, Pat. "Levine, Gail Carson." Silvey, *The Essential Guide to Children's Books and Their Creators*. 261.
   Biographical sketch.

C. S. LEWIS, 1898–1963

Web Sites

"C. S. Lewis Bibliography." *Fantastic Fiction.* 2003. Last accessed 8 Dec. 2003. http://www.fantasticfiction.co.uk/authors/C_S_Lewis.htm.
   List of Lewis's major works.

Liukkonen, Petri. "C(live) S(taples) Lewis." *Author's Calendar*. Ed. Ari Pesonen. 2000. Last accessed 8 Dec. 2003. http://www.kirjasto.sci.fi/cslewis.htm.
Biographical sketch and discussion of Lewis's major works.

Welcome to Narnia. Last accessed 8 Dec. 2003. http://www.narnia.com/.
Official web site. Includes information about Lewis and his Narnia books.

"Zeus, Dr." *Into the Wardrobe: The C. S. Lewis Web Site*. Dec. 2003. Last accessed 8 Dec. 2003. http://cslewis.drzeus.net/.
A well-developed site with biographical sketches and information about Lewis's works.

Biographies and Criticism

Brabander, Jennifer M. "Lewis, C. S." Silvey, *The Essential Guide to Children's Books and Their Creators*. 263–65.
Biographical sketch.

"C(live) S(taples) Lewis." *Children's Literature Review* 27: 104–51.
Biographical sketch, discussion of literary career, excerpts from reviews and commentary.

"Lewis, C(live) S(taples)." *Something About the Author* 100: 155–60.
Biographical sketch with portrait, discussion of major works.

Russell, David L. "C. S. Lewis." Hettinga and Schmidt, *British Children's Writers, 1914–1960* (*Dictionary of Literary Biography* 160): 134–49.
Discussion of literary career and influence.

Bibliographies

"Lewis, C(live) S(taples)." Lynn, *Fantasy Literature for Children and Young Adults*. 770–80.
Lists books and articles about Lewis and his works.

"Lewis, C[live] S[taples]." Hendrickson, *Children's Literature: A Guide to the Criticism*. 171–74.
Lists books and articles about Lewis and his works.

ASTRID LINDGREN, 1907–2002

Web Sites

Astrid Lindgren. Last accessed 8 Dec. 2003. http://www.astridlindgren.se/index_kalender.htm.
Biographical information, including a time line of Lindgren's life. Site available in Swedish, German, and English.

"Astrid Lindgren." *Sweden.se*. Last accessed 8 Dec. 2003. http://www.sweden.se/templates/FactSheet____4402.asp.
From the Swedish government web site. Biographical sketch and list of Lindgren's major works.

"Astrid Lindgren Bibliography." *Fantastic Fiction*. Last accessed 8 Dec. 2003.
http://www.fantasticfiction.co.uk/authors/Astrid_Lindgren.htm.
Lists Lindgren's major works.

Liukkonen, Petri. "Astrid Lindgren." *Author's Calendar*. Ed. Ari Pesonen. 2000.
Last accessed 8 Dec. 2003. http://www.kirjasto.sci.fi/alindgr.htm.
Biographical sketch and discussion of Lindgren's major works.

Biographies and Criticism

"Astrid Lindgren." *Children's Literature Review* 39: 119–65.
Biographical sketch, discussion of literary career, excerpts from reviews
and commentary.

"Lindgren, Astrid." *Something About the Author* 38: 120–35.
Biographical sketch with portrait, discussion of major works.

Russell, David L. "Lindgren, Astrid." Cullinan and Person, *The Continuum Encyclopedia of Children's Literature*. 486–88.
Biographical sketch.

ARNOLD LOBEL, 1933–1987

Web Sites

"Author Spotlight: Arnold Lobel." *HarperCollins*. Last accessed 27 Dec. 2003.
http://www.harpercollins.com/catalog/author_xml.asp?AuthorId=12406.
Biographical sketch.

"Featured Author and Illustrator: Arnold Lobel." *Carol Hurst's Children's Literature Site*. 1999. Last accessed 8 Dec. 2003. http://www.carolhurst.com/
authors/alobel.html.
Biographical sketch.

"Meet Arnold Lobel." *Houghton Mifflin*. 2000. Last accessed 8 Dec. 2003.
http://www.eduplace.com/kids/hmr/mtai/lobel.html.
Publisher web site. Biographical sketch.

Biographies and Criticism

"Arnold Lobel." *Children's Literature Review* 5: 157–76.
Biographical sketch, discussion of literary career, excerpts from reviews
and commentary.

Gmuca, Jacqueline. "Arnold Lobel." Estes, *American Writers for Children Since
1960: Poets, Illustrators, and Nonfiction Authors* (*Dictionary of Literary Biography* 61): 165–76.
Discussion of literary career and influence.

"Lobel, Arnold." *Something About the Author* 55: 88–107.
Biographical sketch with portrait, discussion of major works.

Serafin, Steven R. "Lobel, Arnold." Cullinan and Person, *The Continuum Encyclopedia of Children's Literature*. 494–96.

Shannon, George. *Arnold Lobel*. Boston: Twayne Publishers, 1989.
    Discusses Lobel's literary career and works.

HUGH LOFTING, 1886–1947

Web Sites

"Hugh Lofting." *CORAL (Caribbean Online Resource and Archive)*. 2002. Last accessed 22 Dec. 2003. http://www.caribbeanedu.com/coral/refcen/Biography/readbio.asp?id=143.
    Biographical sketch.

Project Gutenberg. 25 Dec. 2003. Last accessed 27 Dec. 2003. http://www.gutenberg.net/index.shtml.
    Includes uncopyrighted online texts for Lofting's *The Story of Doctor Dolittle* and *Voyages of Dr. Doolittle* (use the "Find an Ebook" link to find texts by Lofting).

Welbourn, Karen W. *Puddleby-on-the-Marsh*. 2003. Last accessed 27 Dec. 2003. http://members.tripod.com/%7EPuddleby/.
    Includes solid biographical information on Lofting and information about his books. Does contain annoying music (which can be turned off) and pop-up ads.

Biographies and Criticism

"Hugh Lofting." *Children's Literature Review* 19: 102–31.
    Biographical sketch, discussion of literary career, excerpts from reviews and commentary.

Imdieke, Sandra. "Lofting, Hugh." Cullinan and Person, *The Continuum Encyclopedia of Children's Literature*. 496–97.
    Biographical sketch.

"Lofting, Hugh (John)." *Something About the Author* 100: 160–63.
    Biographical sketch with portrait, discussion of major works.

Molson, Francis J. "Hugh Lofting." Hettinga and Schmidt, *British Children's Writers, 1914–1960* (*Dictionary of Literary Biography* 160): 150–59.
    Discussion of literary career and influence.

JACK LONDON, 1876–1916

Web Sites

Adler, Jack. "Jack London: The American Karl Marx." *Literary Traveler*. Last accessed 8 Dec. 2003. http://www.literarytraveler.com/jacklondon/jacklondon.htm.
    Biographical sketch.

"Jack London." *CORAL (Caribbean Online Resource and Archive)*. 2002. Last accessed 22 Dec. 2003. http://www.caribbeanedu.com/coral/refcen/Biography/readbio.asp?id=144.
Biographical sketch.

"The Jack London Collection." *Berkeley Digital Library*. 13 Jan. 2003. Last accessed 8 Dec. 2003. http://sunsite.berkeley.edu/London/.
Description of Jack London collection, biographical sketch, and information about London's works.

Project Gutenberg. 25 Dec. 2003. Last accessed 27 Dec. 2003. http://www.gutenberg.net/index.shtml.
Includes uncopyrighted online texts for several of London's works, including *The Call of the Wild* (use the "Find an Ebook" link to find texts by London).

Biographies and Criticism

Lieberman, Craig M. "London, Jack (John Griffith London)." Cullinan and Person, *The Continuum Encyclopedia of Children's Literature*. 497.
Biographical sketch.

Sieruta, Peter D. "London, Jack." Silvey, *Children's Books and Their Creators*. 416–17.
Biographical sketch.

CARLO LORENZINI. *SEE* CARLO COLLODI

LOIS LOWRY, 1937–

Web Sites

"Author Profile: Lois Lowry." *Teenreads.com*. 2003. Last accessed 8 Dec. 2003. http://www.teenreads.com/authors/au-lowry-lois.asp.
Interview from 2000.

Castellitto, Linda M. "Very Interesting People: Lois Lowry." *BookSense.com*. Last accessed 8 Dec. 2003. http://www.booksense.com/people/archive/ lowry.jsp.
Interview with Lowry.

Lois Lowry. Last accessed 8 Dec. 2003. http://www.loislowry.com/.
Author web site. Includes biographical information.

"Lois Lowry." *Kidspace @ The Internet Public Library*. Last accessed 8 Dec. 2003. http://ipl.sils.umich.edu/div/kidspace/askauthor/Lowry.html.
Biographical sketch.

Biographies and Criticism

"Autobiography Feature: Lois Lowry." *Something About the Author* 127: 134–50.
Autobiographical sketch.

Chaston, Joel. *Lois Lowry*. New York: Twayne Publishers, 1997.
Critical commentary on Lowry's works.

Horton, Nancy. "Lowry, Lois." Cullinan and Person, *The Continuum Encyclopedia of Children's Literature*. 499–501.
Biographical sketch.

"Lois Lowry." *Children's Literature Review* 72: 192–206.
Biographical sketch, discussion of literary career, excerpts from reviews and commentary.

Telgen, Diane. "Lowry, Lois." *Something About the Author* 111: 121–28.
Biographical sketch with portrait, discussion of major works.

Zaidman, Laura M. "Lois Lowry." Estes, *American Writers for Children Since 1960: Fiction* (*Dictionary of Literary Biography* 52): 249–61.
Discussion of literary career and influence.

DAVID MACAULAY, 1946–

Web Sites

"David Macaulay." *Kidsread.com*. Last accessed 10 Dec. 2003. http://www.kidsreads.com/authors/au-macaulay-david.asp.
Biographical sketch.

Biographies and Criticism

"David (Alexander) Macaulay." *Children's Literature Review* 14: 162–76.
Biographical sketch, discussion of literary career, excerpts from reviews and commentary.

Eutsler, Nellvena Duncan. "David Macaulay." Estes, *American Writers for Children Since 1960: Poets, Illustrators, and Nonfiction Authors* (*Dictionary of Literary Biography* 52): 177–88.
Discussion of literary career and influence.

"Macaulay, David (Alexander)." *Something About the Author* 137: 128–35.
Biographical sketch with portrait, discussion of major works.

Silvey, Anita. "Macaulay, David." Silvey, *The Essential Guide to Children's Books and Their Creators*. 277–79.
Biographical sketch.

GEORGE MACDONALD, 1824–1905

Web Sites

Blakemore, Ian P. *The Golden Key*. 9 Nov. 2003. Last accessed 9 Dec. 2003. http://www.ev90481.dial.pipex.com/.

Extensive site. Includes biographical information on MacDonald, as well as information about his works and links to related sites.

"George MacDonald." *CORAL (Caribbean Online Resource and Archive)*. 2002. Last accessed 22 Dec. 2003. http://www.caribbeanedu.com/coral/refcen/ Biography/readbio.asp?id=148.
Biographical sketch.

"George MacDonald Bibliography." *Fantastic Fiction*. 2003. Last accessed 9 Dec. 2003. http://www.fantasticfiction.co.uk/authors/George_MacDonald .htm.
Lists MacDonald's major works.

Montag, Linda. "Subversion and Recuperation of Gender Roles in George Mac- Donald's 'The Day Boy and the Night Girl.' " *The Looking Glass* 7: 4 (2 Jan. 2003). Last accessed 9 Dec. 2003. http://www.the-looking-glass.net/rabbit/ v7i1/academy.
Critical essay.

Project Gutenberg. 25 Dec. 2003. Last accessed 27 Dec. 2003. http://www .gutenberg.net/index.shtml.
Includes uncopyrighted online texts for several of MacDonald's works, in- cluding *At the Back of the North Wind* and *The Princess and the Goblins* (use the "Find an Ebook" link to find texts by MacDonald).

Robb, David S. "George MacDonald." *Scottish Authors*. 1 Jul. 2000. http://www .slainte.org.uk/Scotauth/macdodsw.htm.
Short biographical piece.

Biographies and Criticism

"George MacDonald." *Children's Literature Review* 67: 111–46.
Biographical sketch, discussion of literary career, excerpts from reviews and commentary.

"MacDonald, George." *Something About the Author* 100: 166–71.
Biographical sketch with portrait, discussion of major works.

May, Jill P. "MacDonald, George." Silvey, *The Essential Guide to Children's Books and Their Creators*. 280–81.
Biographical sketch.

McGillis, Roderick. "George MacDonald." Khorana, *British Children's Writers, 1800–1880 (Dictionary of Literary Biography* 163): 183–93.
Discussion of literary career and influence.

Bibliographies

"MacDonald, George." Hendrickson, *Children's Literature: A Guide to the Criti- cism*. 185–87.
Lists books and articles about MacDonald.

ANNE McCAFFREY, 1926–

Web Sites

"Anne McCaffrey." *sffworld.com.* 2003. Last accessed 9 Dec. 2003. http://www.sffworld.com/authors/m/mccaffrey_anne/index.html.
Includes brief biographical sketch, primary bibliography, and a link to an 2000 sffworld.com interview with McCaffrey.

"The Anne McCaffrey Archives." *Random House.* Last accessed 9 Dec. 2003. http://www.randomhouse.com/delrey/pern/amcc/index.html.
Publisher web site. Includes information about McCaffrey's works and her life.

"Anne McCaffrey Bibliography." *Fantastic Fiction.* 2003. Last accessed 9 Dec. 2003. http://www.fantasticfiction.co.uk/authors/Anne_McCaffrey.htm.
Lists McCaffrey's major works.

"Interview with Anne McCaffrey." *Wired for Books.* Last accessed 9 Dec. 2003. http://wiredforbooks.org/annemccaffrey/.
Includes audio files from 1988 interview with McCaffrey.

The Worlds of Anne McCaffrey. 11 Oct. 2003. Last accessed 9 Dec. 2003. http://www.annemccaffrey.org/.
Author web site. Includes biographical information.

Biographies and Criticism

"Anne (Inez) McCaffrey." *Children's Literature Review* 49: 133–58.
Biographical sketch, discussion of literary career, excerpts from reviews and commentary.

Deifendeifer, Anne E. "McCaffrey, Anne." Silvey, *The Essential Guide to Children's Books and Their Creators*: 290–91.
Biographical sketch.

Jones, J. Sydney. "Anne McCaffrey." *Authors and Artists for Young Adults* 34: 141–50.
Biographical sketch with portrait, discussion of major works. Includes primary and secondary bibliographies.

Bibliographies

"McCaffrey, Anne (Inez)." Lynn, *Fantasy Literature for Children and Young Adults*. 788–89.
Lists books and articles about McCaffrey and her works.

ROBERT McCLOSKEY, 1914–2003

Web Sites

"McCloskey, Robert." *Educational Paperback Association*. Last accessed 9 Dec. 2003. http://www.edupaperback.org/showauth.cfm?authid=35.
Biographical sketch with selected list of major works.

"Robert McCloskey." *The Scoop*. Last accessed 9 Dec. 2003. http://www.friend .ly.net/scoop/biographies/mccloskeyrobert/index.html.
Biographical sketch with portrait.

Silvey, Anita. "Robert McCloskey interviewed by Anita Silvey." *The Horn Book*. Last accessed 9 Dec. 2003. http://www.hbook.com/exhibit/mccloskeyradio .html.
Audio files from interview with McCloskey.

Biographies and Criticism

Fannin, Alice. "Robert McCloskey." Cech, *American Writers for Children, 1900–1960* (*Dictionary of Literary Biography* 22): 259–66.
Discussion of literary career and influence.

"John (Robert) McCloskey." *Children's Literature Review* 7: 189–211.
Biographical sketch, discussion of literary career, excerpts from reviews and commentary.

Lipsitt, Judy. "McCloskey, Robert." Cullinan and Person, *The Continuum Encyclopedia of Children's Literature*. 529–31.
Biographical sketch.

"McCloskey, (John) Robert." *Something About the Author* 100: 171–75.
Biographical sketch with portrait, discussion of major works.

Schmidt, Gary D. *Robert McCloskey*. Boston: Twayne Publishers, 1990.
Critical commentary on McCloskey's works.

ROBIN McKINLEY, 1952–

Web Sites

Robin McKinley. 3 Nov. 2003. Last accessed 10 Dec. 2003. http://www.robin mckinley.com/.
Author web site. Includes biographical information.

"Robin McKinley." *Fantastic Fiction*. 2003. Last accessed 10 Dec. 2003. http://www.fantasticfiction.co.uk/authors/Robin_McKinley.htm.
Lists McKinley's major works.

Sanders, Lynn. " 'Girls Who Do Things': The Protagonists of Robin McKinley's Fantasy Fiction." *ALAN Review* 24: 1 (Fall 1996). Last accessed 10 Dec.

2003. http://scholar.lib.vt.edu/ejournals/ALAN/fall96/f96-08-Sanders. html. Critical essay.

Biographies and Criticism

"(Jennifer Carolyn) Robin McKinley." *Children's Literature Review* 81: 180–90.
    Biographical sketch, discussion of literary career, excerpts from reviews and commentary.

Karrenbrock, Marilyn H. "Robin McKinley." Estes, *American Writers for Children Since 1960: Fiction* (*Dictionary of Literary Biography* 52): 262–66.
    Discussion of literary career and influence.

"McKinley, Robin." *Authors and Artists for Young Adults* 33: 131–36.
    Biographical sketch with portrait, discussion of major works.

West, Jane. "McKinley, Robin." Cullinan and Person, *The Continuum Encyclopedia of Children's Literature*. 536–37.
    Biographical sketch.

A. A. MILNE, 1882–1956

Web Sites

"A. A. Milne." *BBC Books*. Last accessed 10 Dec. 2003. http://www.bbc.co.uk/arts/books/author/milne/.
    Portrait, biographical sketch, list of important works.

"A. A. Milne." *Kidsread.com*. 2000. Last accessed 10 Dec. 2003. http://www.kidsreads.com/authors/au-milne-aa.asp.
    Biographical sketch.

"Alan Alexander Milne." *CORAL (Caribbean Online Resource and Archive)*. 2002. Last accessed 22 Dec. 2003. http://www.caribbeanedu.com/coral/refcen/Biography/readbio.asp?id=165.
    Biographical sketch.

Liukkonen, Petri. "A(lan) A(lexander) Milne." *Author's Calendar*. Ed. Ari Pesonen. 2000. Last accessed 10 Dec. 2003. http://www.kirjasto.sci.fi/aamilne.htm.
    Biographical sketch and discussion of Milne's major works.

Milne, James. *The Page at Pooh Corner*. 28 Aug. 2003. Last accessed 10 Dec. 2003. http://www.pooh-corner.org/.
    Extensive site. Includes biographical sketch, time line, information about Milne's works.

Biographies and Criticism

"A(lan) A(lexander) Milne." *Children's Literature Review* 26: 126–71.
    Biographical sketch, discussion of literary career, excerpts from reviews and commentary.

Lengel, Carolyn J. "Milne, A(lan) A(lexander)." Cullinan and Person, *The Continuum Encyclopedia of Children's Literature*. 548–49.
Biographical sketch.

"Milne, A(lan) A(lexander)." *Something About the Author* 100: 175–80.
Biographical sketch with portrait, discussion of major works.

Otten, Charlotte F. "A. A. Milne." Hettinga and Schmidt, *British Children's Writers, 1914–1960* (*Dictionary of Literary Biography* 160): 177–88.
Discussion of literary career and influence.

Bibliographies

"Milne, A. A." Hendrickson, *Children's Literature: A Guide to the Criticism*. 195–97.
Lists books and articles about Milne and his works.

ELSE HOLMELUND MINARIK, 1920–

"Else H. Minarik." *HarperChildrens.com*. Last accessed 10 Dec. 2003. http://www.harperchildrens.com/authorintro/index.asp?authorid=12489.
Publisher web site. Includes a biographical sketch.

Walters, John. "Else Minarik and The Little Bear Series." *The Front Porch (New Hampshire Public Radio)*. 10 Sept. 2003. Last accessed 10 Dec. 2003. http://nhpr.org/view_content/5130/.
Audio file of 2003 interview.

Biographies and Criticism

"Else Holmelund Minarik." *Children's Literature Review* 33: 120–28.
Biographical sketch, discussion of literary career, excerpts from reviews and commentary.

"Minarik, Else Holmelund." *Something About the Author* 127: 158–61.
Biographical sketch with portrait, discussion of major works.

Riley, Patricia. "Minarik, Else Holmelund." Silvey, *The Essential Guide to Children's Books and Their Creators*. 306–7.
Biographical sketch.

L. M. MONTGOMERY, 1874–1942

Web Sites

Liukkonen, Petri. "L. M. Montgomery." *Author's Calendar*. Ed. Ari Pesonen. 2000. Last accessed 10 Dec. 2003. http://www.kirjasto.sci.fi/lmmontg.htm.
Biographical sketch and discussion of Montgomery's major works.

L. M. Montgomery in Rainbow Island: A Resource Guide. 18 Sept. 2003. Last accessed 10 Dec. 2003. http://www.geocities.com/valancy8/LMM .html.
Includes biographical sketch, links to similar online resources.

"Lucy Maud Montgomery." *CORAL (Caribbean Online Resource and Archive).* 2002. Last accessed 22 Dec. 2003. http://www.caribbeanedu.com/coral/ refcen/Biography/readbio.asp?id=167.
Biographical sketch.

Murphy, Joanne V. "Lucy Maud Montgomery: An Island Tribute to a Great Writer." *The Literary Traveler.* 2003. Last accessed 10 Dec. 2003. http:// www.literarytraveler.com/montgomery/lucymaud.htm.
Biographical sketch.

Project Gutenberg. 25 Dec. 2003. Last accessed 27 Dec. 2003. http://www .gutenberg.net/index.shtml.
Includes uncopyrighted online texts for several of Montgomery's works, including *Anne of Green Gables* (use the "Find an Ebook" link to find texts by Montgomery).

Biographies and Criticism

Cavert, Beth. "Montgomery, L. M. (Lucy Maud)." Cullinan and Person, *The Continuum Encyclopedia of Children's Literature.* 553–55.
Biographical sketch.

"L(ucy) M(aud) Montgomery." *Children's Literature Review* 8: 107–40.
Biographical sketch, discussion of literary career, excerpts from reviews and commentary.

"Montgomery, L(ucy) M(aud)." *Something About the Author* 100: 180–84.
Biographical sketch with portrait, discussion of major works.

Bibliographies

"Montgomery, Lucy Maud." Hendrickson, *Children's Literature: A Guide to the Criticism.* 198–99.
Lists books and articles about Montgomery and her works.

PAT MORA, 1942–

Web Sites

Pat Mora. Last accessed 10 Dec. 2003. http://www.patmora.com/.
Author web site. Includes biographical information.

"Pat Mora." *Academy of American Poets.* 17 July 2000. Last accessed 10 Dec. 2003. http://www.poets.org/poets/poets.cfm?prmID=297.
Biographical sketch, selected bibliography, links to related sites.

"Pat Mora." *Penguin Group (USA)*. 2003. Last accessed 10 Dec. 2003. http://www.penguinputnam.com/Author/AuthorFrame/?0000018319.
Short biographical sketch.

Reuben, Paul P. "Chapter 10: Late Twentieth Century—Pat Mora (1942–)." *PAL: Perspectives in American Literature—A Research and Reference Guide*. 9 Jan. 2003. Last accessed 10 Dec. 2003. http://www.csustan.edu/english/reuben/pal/chap10/mora.html.
Includes primary and secondary bibliographies, portrait, links to related sites.

Biographies and Criticism

Broughton, Mary Ariail. "Mora, Pat." Cullinan and Person, *The Continuum Encyclopedia of Children's Literature*. 557.
Biographical sketch.

Kanellos, Nicolás. "Pat Mora." Lomeli, Francisco A., and Carl R. Shirley, eds. *Chicano Writers, Third Series* (*Dictionary of Literary Biography* 209): 160–63. Detroit, MI: Gale, 1999.
Discussion of literary career and influence.

"Pat(ricia) Mora." *Children's Literature Review* 58: 130–43.
Biographical sketch, discussion of literary career, excerpts from reviews and commentary.

Senick, Gerard. "Mora, Pat(ricia)." *Something About the Author* 134: 110–18.
Biographical sketch with portrait, discussion of major works.

WALTER DEAN MYERS, 1937–

Web Sites

"Myers, Walter Dean." *Educational Paperback Association*. Last accessed 10 Dec. 2003. http://www.edupaperback.org/showauth.cfm?authid=63.
Biographical sketch with list of major works.

"Walter Dean Myers." *Houghton Mifflin*. 2000. Last accessed 10 Dec. 2003. http://www.eduplace.com/kids/hmr/mtai/wdmyers.html.
Biographical profile.

"Walter Dean Myers." *Teenreads.com*. 2003. Last accessed 10 Dec. 2003. http://www.teenreads.com/authors/au-myers-walterdean.asp.
Biographical profile.

Biographies and Criticism

Senick, Gerard J. "Myers, Walter Dean." *Something About the Author* 109: 163–72.
Biographical sketch with portrait, discussion of major works.

"Walter Dean Myers." *Children's Literature Review* 35: 173–206.
Biographical sketch, discussion of literary career, excerpts from reviews and commentary.

Wilson, Nance S. "Myers, Walter Dean." Cullinan and Person, *The Continuum Encyclopedia of Children's Literature*. 571–72.
Biographical sketch.

F. OGDEN NASH, 1902–1971

Web Sites

"Ogden Nash." *Academy of American Poets*. 25 Apr. 2001. Last accessed 10 Dec. 2003. http://www.poets.org/poets/poets.cfm?prmID=690.
Biographical sketch, selected bibliography, links to related sites.

"Ogden Nash." *BBC*. Last accessed 10 Dec. 2003. http://www.bbc.co.uk/bbcfour/audiointerviews/profilepages/nasho2.shtml.
Portrait, clips from 1964 interview, brief biographical sketch, links to other sites of interest.

"Ogden Nash." *BBC Books*. Last accessed 10 Dec. 2003. http://www.bbc.co.uk/arts/books/author/nash/.
Portrait, biographical sketch, list of major works.

"Ogden Nash." *University of Texas Harry Ransom Humanities Research Center*. Last accessed 10 Dec. 2003. http://www.lib.utexas.edu/taro/uthrc/00098/hrc-00098.html#a2.
Description of Ogden Nash materials at the Harry Ransom Humanities Research Center. Includes a biographical sketch.

Biographies and Criticism

Kvilhaug, Sarah Guille. "Nash, Ogden." Silvey, *Children's Books and Their Creators*. 481–82.

"Nash, (Frederic) Ogden." *Something About the Author* 46: 162–77.
Biographical sketch with portrait, discussion of major works.

"Ogden Nash." *Twentieth-Century Literature Criticism* 109: 353–67.
Discussion of literary career, discussion of critical commentary on Nash's works.

EDITH NESBIT, 1858–1924

Web Sites

"Edith Nesbit." *CORAL (Caribbean Online Resource and Archive)*. 2002. Last accessed 22 Dec. 2003. http://www.caribbeanedu.com/coral/refcen/Biography/readbio.asp?id=175.
Biographical sketch.

"Edith Nesbit Bibliography." *Fantastic Fiction.* 2003. Last accessed 10 Dec. 2003. http://www.fantasticfiction.co.uk/authors/Edith_Nesbit.htm. Lists Nesbit's major works.

Gaipa, Mark. "E[dith] Nesbit." *The Modernist Journals Project.* Sept. 1999. Last accessed 10 Dec. 2003. http://www.modjourn.brown.edu/mjp/Bios/Nesbit.html. Biographical sketch.

Project Gutenberg. 25 Dec. 2003. Last accessed 27 Dec. 2003. http://www.gutenberg.net/index.shtml.
Includes uncopyrighted online texts for several of Nesbit's works, including *Five Children and It* (use the "Find an Ebook" link to find texts by Nesbit).

Biographies and Criticism

"E. Nesbit." *Children's Literature Review* 70: 97–223.
Biographical sketch, discussion of literary career, excerpts from reviews and commentary.

Gilbertson, Irvyn G. "Nesbit, Edith." Cullinan and Person, *The Continuum Encyclopedia of Children's Literature.* 582–84.
Biographical sketch.

Nelson, Claudia. "E. Nesbit." Zaidman, *British Children's Writers, 1880–1914* (*Dictionary of Literary Biography* 141): 199–216.
Discussion of literary career and influence.

"Nesbit, E(dith)." *Something About the Author* 100: 185–89.
Biographical sketch with portrait, discussion of major works.

Bibliographies

"Nesbit (Bland), E(dith)." Lynn, *Fantasy Literature for Children and Young Adults.* 814–17.
List of books and articles about Nesbit and her works.

"Nesbit, E. [Edith Nesbit Bland]." Hendrickson, *Children's Literature: A Guide to the Criticism.* 201–3.
Lists books and articles about Nesbit and her works.

ANDRE NORTON, 1912–

Web Sites

Andre Norton. 25 Aug. 2003. Last accessed 10 Dec. 2003. http://www.andre-norton.org/.
Official web site; includes biographical material.

"Andre Norton." *CORAL (Caribbean Online Resource and Archive).* 2002. Last accessed 22 Dec. 2003. http://www.caribbeanedu.com/coral/refcen/Biography/readbio.asp?id=178.
Biographical sketch.

"Andre Norton Bibliography." *Fantastic Fiction*. 2003. Last accessed 10 Dec. 2003. http://www.fantasticfiction.co.uk/authors/Andre_Norton.htm. List of Norton's major works.

Cornwell, J. M. "Andre Norton: An interview." *The Rose & Thorn*. Last accessed 10 Dec. 2003. http://members.aol.com/Raven763/andrenorton.html. Interview with Norton.

Biographies and Criticism

"Andre Norton." *Children's Literature Review* 50: 128–64.
Biographical sketch, discussion of literary career, excerpts from reviews and commentary.

James, J. Alison. "Norton, Andre." Silvey, *The Essential Guide to Children's Books and Their Creators*. 327–28.
Biographical sketch.

Jones, J. Sydney. "Norton, Andre." *Something About the Author* 91: 148–56.
Biographical sketch with portrait, discussion of major works.

Molson, Francis J. "Andre Norton (Alice Mary Norton)." Estes, *American Writers for Children Since 1960: Fiction* (*Dictionary of Literary Biography* 52): 267–78.
Discussion of literary career and influence.

Bibliographies

"Norton, Andre (Alice Mary Norton)." Hendrickson, *Children's Literature: A Guide to the Criticism*. 204–5.
Lists books and articles about Norton and her works.

MARY NORTON, 1903–1992

Web Sites

"Mary Norton." *CORAL (Caribbean Online Resource and Archive)*. 2002. Last accessed 22 Dec. 2003. http://www.caribbeanedu.com/coral/refcen/Biography/readbio.asp?id=179.
Biographical sketch.

"Mary Norton: Author and Creator of 'The Borrowers.' " *The Leighton- Linslade Home Page*. Last accessed 10 Dec. 2003. http://www.leighton-linslade.org.uk/Mary%20Norton/biog.htm.
Biographical sketch.

"Mary Norton Bibliography." *Fantastic Fiction*. 2003. Last accessed 10 Dec. 2003. http://www.fantasticfiction.co.uk/authors/Mary_Norton.htm.
Lists Norton's major works.

Biographies and Criticism

Ash, Gwynne Ellen. "Norton, Mary." Cullinan and Person, *The Continuum Encyclopedia of Children's Literature*. 596.
Biographical sketch.

"Mary Norton." *Children's Literature Review* 6: 210–27.
Biographical sketch, discussion of literary career, excerpts from reviews and commentary.

"Norton, Mary." *Something About the Author* 60: 101–10.
Biographical sketch with portrait, discussion of major works.

Scott, Jon C. "Mary Norton." Hettinga and Schmidt, *British Children's Writers, 1914–1960* (*Dictionary of Literary Biography* 160): 197–206.
Discussion of literary career and influence.

ROBERT C. O'BRIEN, 1918–1973

Web Sites

"Robert C. O'Brien." *Fantastic Fiction*. 2003. 10 Dec. 2003. http://www.fantasticfiction.co.uk/authors/Robert_C_OBrien.htm.
Lists O'Brien's major works.

"Robert O'Brien." *CORAL (Caribbean Online Resource and Archive)*. 2002. Last accessed 22 Dec. 2003. http://www.caribbeanedu.com/coral/refcen/Biography/ readbio.asp?id=181.
Biographical sketch.

Biographies and Criticism

Imdieke, Sandra. "O'Brien, Robert C. (Robert Leslie Conly)." Cullinan and Person, *The Continuum Encyclopedia of Children's Literature*. 598.
Biographical sketch.

"O'Brien, Robert C." *Children's Literature Review* 2: 127–30.
Biographical sketch, discussion of literary career, excerpts from reviews and commentary.

"Robert O'Brien." *Authors and Artists for Young Adults* 6: 173–80.
Biographical sketch with portrait, discussion of major works.

Sieruta, Peter D. "O'Brien, Robert C." Silvey, *The Essential Guide to Children's Books and Their Creators*. 331–32.
Biographical sketch.

SCOTT O'DELL, 1898–1989

Web Sites

Hall, H. R. *Scott O'Dell*. 30 Sept. 2003. Last accessed 10 Dec. 2003. http://www.scottodell.com/.
Includes a Biographical sketch.

"O'Dell, Scott." *Educational Paperback Association*. Last accessed 10 Dec. 2003. http://www.edupaperback.org/showauth.cfm?authid=65.
Biographical sketch with list of major works.

"Scott O'Dell." *CORAL (Caribbean Online Resource and Archive)*. 2002. Last accessed 22 Dec. 2003. http://www.caribbeanedu.com/coral/refcen/Biography/readbio.asp?id=182.
Biographical sketch.

Biographies and Criticism

Jones, J. Sydney. "Scott O'Dell." *Authors and Artists for Young Adults* 44: 159–68.
Biographical sketch with portrait, discussion of major works.

Russell, David L. *Scott O'Dell*. New York: Twayne Publishers, 1999.
Critical commentary on O'Dell's works.

"Scott O'Dell." *Children's Literature Review* 16: 159–80.
Biographical sketch, discussion of literary career, excerpts from reviews and commentary.

Sieruta, Peter D. "O'Dell, Scott." Silvey, *The Essential Guide to Children's Books and Their Creators*. 332–33.
Biographical sketch.

Usrey, Malcolm. "Scott O'Dell." Estes, *American Writers for Children Since 1960: Fiction (Dictionary of Literary Biography* 52): 278–95.
Discussion of literary career and influence.

Bibliographies

"O'Dell, Scott." Hendrickson, *Children's Literature: A Guide to the Criticism*. 206–7.
Lists books and articles about O'Dell and his works.

KATHERINE PATERSON, 1932–

Web Sites

"Katherine Paterson." *KidSpace @ the Internet Public Library*. Last accessed 10 Dec. 2003. http://ipl.si.umich.edu/div/kidspace/askauthor/paterson.html.
Biographical profile.

"Katherine Paterson." *Kidsreads.com.* 2000. Last accessed 10 Dec. 2003. http://www.kidsreads.com/authors/au-paterson-katherine.asp.
Biographical sketch.

Katherine Paterson Official Web Site. 2003. Last accessed 10 Dec. 2003. http://www.terabithia.com/.
Author web site. Includes biographical information.

Liddie, Patricia A. "Vision of Self in Katherine Paterson's *Jacob Have I Loved.*" *ALAN Review* 21: 3 (Spring 1994). Last accessed 10 Dec. 2003. http://scholar.lib.vt.edu/ejournals/ALAN/spring94/Liddie.html.
Critical essay.

Paterson, Katherine, and Virginia Buckley. "An Author and Editor Look at the Creative Process." *Cooperative Children's Book Center, School of Education, University of Wisconsin-Madison.* Last accessed 23 Dec. 2003. http://media.education.wisc.edu:8080/ramgen/ccbc/ibby1999five.rm.
Online video of a presentation given by Katherine Paterson and her editor, Virginia Buckley, at the Third Biennial International Board on Books for Young People Regional Conference, in Madison, Wisconsin, on October 8–9, 1999 (Joan Glazer, who appears first in the video, introduced them).

Biographies and Criticism

Edwards, Eden K. "Paterson, Katherine." Silvey, *The Essential Guide to Children's Books and Their Creators.* 340–41.
Biographical sketch.

"Katherine (Womeldrof) Paterson." *Children's Literature Review* 50: 165–207.
Biographical sketch, discussion of literary career, excerpts from reviews and commentary.

Senick, Gerard J. "Paterson, Katherine." *Something About the Author* 133: 134–44.
Biographical sketch with portrait, discussion of major works.

Smedman, M. Sarah. "Katherine Paterson." Estes, *American Writers for Children Since 1960: Fiction* (*Dictionary of Literary Biography* 52): 296–314.
Discussion of literary career and influence.

Smedman, M. Sarah, and Joel D. Chaston, eds. *Bridges for the Young: The Fiction of Katherine Paterson.* Lanham, MD: Children's Literature Association and Scarecrow Press, 2003.
Book-length study of Paterson and her literary career.

Bibliographies

"Paterson, Kathrine." Hendrickson, *Children's Literature: A Guide to the Criticism.* 208–10.
Lists books and articles about Paterson.

JILL (GILLIAN) PATON WALSH, 1937–

Web Sites

Jill Paton Walsh. Last accessed 10 Dec. 2003. http://www.greenbay.co.uk/jpw
.html.
Author web site on publisher web site. Includes biographical information.

Biographies and Criticism

Donahue, Rosanne Fraine. "Jill Paton Walsh." Hunt, *British Children's Writers Since 1960* (*Dictionary of Literary Biography* 161): 245–57.
Discussion of literary career and influence.

Gilbertson, Irvyn G. "Paton Walsh, Jill." Cullinan and Person, *The Continuum Encyclopedia of Children's Literature*. 612–14.
Biographical sketch.

"Jill Paton Walsh." *Children's Literature Review* 65: 154–90.
Biographical sketch, discussion of literary career, excerpts from reviews and commentary.

Senick, Gerard J. "Paton Walsh, Gillian (Jill Paton Walsh)." *Something About the Author* 109: 180–89.
Biographical sketch, discussion of major works.

RICHARD PECK, 1934–

Web Sites

Castellitto, Linda. "Lessons Learned: Former Teacher Richard Peck Educates and Entertains with 'River.'" *BookPage*. 2003. Last accessed 10 Dec. 2003. http://www.bookpage.com/0310bp/richard_peck.html.
Interview with Peck.

"Richard Peck." *Penguin Group (USA)*. 2000. Last accessed 10 Dec. 2003. http://www.penguinputnam.com/Author/AuthorFrame?0000020017.
Biographical sketch.

"Richard Peck Papers." *de Grummond Collection*. July 2001. Last accessed 10 Dec. 2003. http://www.lib.usm.edu/%7Edegrum/html/research/findaids/ peck.htm.
Description of Richard Peck archival papers at the de Grummond Collection. Includes Biographical sketch, discussion of major works.

Biographies and Criticism

"Autobiography Feature: Richard Peck." *Something About the Author* 110: 159–70.
Autobiographical sketch.

Durham, Irene. "Richard Peck." *Authors and Artists for Young Adults* 24: 151–61.
Biographical sketch with portrait, discussion of major works.

Jones, Patrick, and Peter D. Sieruta. "Peck, Richard." Silvey, *The Essential Guide to Children's Books and Their Creators*. 344–45.
    Biographical sketch.

"Richard Peck." *Children's Literature Review* 15: 146–66.
    Biographical sketch, discussion of literary career, excerpts from reviews and commentary.

ROBERT NEWTON PECK, 1928–

Web Sites

"Author Tracker: Robert Newton Peck." *HarperCollins*. Last accessed 27 Dec. 2003. http://www.harpercollins.com/catalog/author_xml.asp?AuthorId= 13828.
    Short biographical sketch.

Robert Newton Peck. 15 July 2002. Last accessed 27 Dec. 2003. http:// my.athenet.net/%7Eblahnik/rnpeck/.
    Author's home page. Includes biographical information.

Biographies and Criticism

"Robert Newton Peck." *Authors and Artists for Young Adults* 43: 153–62.
    Biographical sketch with portrait, discussion of major works.

"Robert Newton Peck." *Children's Literature Review* 45: 93–126.
    Biographical sketch, discussion of literary career, excerpts from reviews and commentary.

Russell, David L. "Peck, Robert Newton." Cullinan and Person, *The Continuum Encyclopedia of Children's Literature*. 618.
    Biographical sketch.

DANIEL PINKWATER, 1941–

Web Sites

Aileron, *The P-Zone*. 2003. Last accessed 11 Dec. 2003. http://pinkwater.com/ pzone/.
    Extensive site devoted to Pinkwater. Includes biographical information.

"Daniel Manus Pinkwater." *Fantastic Fiction*. 2003. Last accessed 11 Dec. 2003. http://www.fantasticfiction.co.uk/authors/Daniel_M_Pinkwater.htm.
    Lists Pinkwater's major works.

"Daniel Pinkwater." *KidSpace @ The Internet Public Library*. Last accessed 11 Dec. 2003. http://ipl.sils.umich.edu/div/kidspace/askauthor/Pinkwater. html.
    Biographical sketch and interview with Pinkwater.

Biographies and Criticism

"D(aniel) Manus Pinkwater." *Children's Literature Review* 4: 161–71.
Biographical sketch, discussion of literary career, excerpts from reviews and commentary.

"Daniel Pinkwater." *Authors and Artists for Young Adults* 46: 145–55.
Biographical sketch with portrait, discussion of major works.

Heppermann, Christine M. "Pinkwater, Daniel." Silvey, *The Essential Guide to Children's Books and Their Creators*. 356–57.
Biographical sketch.

EDGAR ALLAN POE, 1809–1849

Web Sites

"Edgar Allan Poe." *Fantastic Fiction*. 2003. Last accessed 11 Dec. 2003. http://www.fantasticfiction.co.uk/authors/Edgar_Allan_Poe.htm.
List of Poe's major works.

"Edgar Allan Poe." *University of Texas Harry Ransome Humanities Research Center*. Last accessed 11 Dec. 2003. http://www.lib.utexas.edu/taro/uthrc/00109/hrc-00109.html.
Description of Poe archival materials at the Harry Ransome Humanities Research Center. Includes biographical sketch.

The Edgar Allan Poe Society of Baltimore. 23 May 2003. Last accessed 11 Dec. 2003. http://www.eapoe.org/.
Extensive site. Includes information on Poe's life and works.

Project Gutenberg. 25 Dec. 2003. Last accessed 27 Dec. 2003. http://www.gutenberg.net/index.shtml.
Includes uncopyrighted online texts for several of Poe's works, including *The Fall of the House of Usher* (use the "Find an Ebook" link to find texts by Poe).

Reuben, Paul P. "Chapter 3: Early Nineteenth Century—Edgar Allan Poe (1809–1849)." *PAL: Perspectives in American Literature—A Research and Reference Guide*. 4 Dec. 2003. Last accessed 11 Dec. 2003. http://www.csustan.edu/english/reuben/pal/chap3/poe.html.
Includes primary and secondary bibliographies, portrait, links to related sites.

Biographies and Criticism

Carlson, Eric W. "Edgar Allan Poe." Kimbel, Bobby Ellen, and William E. Grant, eds. *American Short-Story Writers Before 1880* (*Dictionary of Literary Biography* 74): 303–22. Detroit, MI: Gale, 1988.
Discussion of Poe's literary career, focusing on his short stories.

May, Charles E. *Edgar Allan Poe: A Study of the Short Fiction*. Boston: Twayne Publishers, 1991.
Book-length study of Poe and his short fiction.

Pendergast, Tom. "Edgar Allan Poe." *Authors and Artists for Young Adults* 14: 189–201.
Biographical sketch with portrait, discussion of major works.

Dictionaries, Encyclopedias, and Handbooks

Carlson, Eric W. *A Companion to Poe Studies*. Westport, CT: Greenwood, 1996.
Includes Information about Poe's literary career and critical reception.

BEATRIX POTTER, 1866–1943

Web Sites

"Beatrix Potter." *BBC h2g2*. Last accessed 11 Dec. 2003. http://www.bbc.co.uk/dna/h2g2/alabaster/A642151.
Biographical sketch.

Liukkonen, Petri. "Beatrix Potter." *Author's Calendar*. Ed. Ari Pesonen. 2000. Last accessed 11 Dec. 2003. http://www.kirjasto.sci.fi/bpotter.htm.
Biographical sketch and discussion of Potter's major works.

Ortakales, Denise. "Beatrix Potter." *Women Children's Illustrators*. Last accessed 11 Dec. 2003. http://www.ortakales.com/illustrators/.
Biographical article with portrait, illustrations.

Straw, Deborah. "More than Just Bunnies: The Legacy of Beatrix Potter." *The Literary Traveler*. 2003. Last accessed 11 Dec. 2003. http://www.literarytraveler.com/europe/potter.htm.
Biographical sketch.

World of Peter Rabbit. 2002. Last accessed 11 Dec. 2003. http://www.peterrabbit.com/.
Official web site. Includes biographical information about Potter.

Biographies and Criticism

"Beatrix Potter." *Children's Literature Review* 73: 126–232.
Biographical sketch, discussion of literary career, excerpts from reviews and commentary.

Kutzer, M. Daphne. *Beatrix Potter: Writing in Code*. New York: Routledge, 2003.
Critical commentary on Potter's works. Includes a bibliography of works by and about Potter.

Lengel, Carolyn. "Potter, (Helen) Beatrix (Heelis)." Cullinan and Person, *The Continuum Encyclopedia of Children's Literature*. 639–41.
Biographical sketch.

MacDonald, Ruth K. "Beatrix Potter." Zaidman, *British Children's Writers, 1880–1914* (*Dictionary of Literary Biography* 141): 230–48.
　　Discussion of literary career and influence.

"Potter, (Helen) Beatrix." *Something About the Author* 132: 177–82.
　　Biographical sketch with portrait, discussion of major works.

Bibliographies

"Potter, Beatrix." Hendrickson, *Children's Literature: A Guide to the Criticism.* 216–21.
　　Lists books and articles about Potter and her works.

PHILIP PULLMAN, 1946–

Web Sites

Abbots, Jennifer. "Author Profile: Philip Pullman." *Teenreads.com.* 2003. Last accessed 11 Dec. 2003. http://www.teenreads.com/authors/au-pullman-philip .asp.
　　Biographical sketch; interview.

"His Dark Materials." *Random House.* 2003. Last accessed 11 Dec. 2003. http://www.randomhouse.com/features/pullman/.
　　Publisher web site. Includes information on Pullman and his Dark Materials trilogy.

His Dark Materials (an unofficial fansite). Last accessed 11 Dec. 2003. http://www.darkmaterials.com/pull.htm.
　　Extensive web site. Includes information on Pullman and his books, as well as links to related sites.

"Philip Pullman." *BBC Books.* Last accessed 11 Dec. 2003. http://www.bbc.co .uk/arts/books/author/pullman/.
　　Includes portrait, biographical and literary sketch, list of major works, links of interest.

Welch, Dave. "Philip Pullman Reaches the Garden." *Powells.com.* 2000. Last accessed 11 Dec. 2003. http://www.powells.com/authors/pullman.html.
　　Interview with Pullman.

Biographies and Criticism

Deifendeifer, Anne E., and Maria B. Salvadore. "Pullman, Philip." Silvey, *The Essential Guide to Children's Books and Their Creators.* 371–72.
　　Biographical sketch.

"Philip Pullman." *Children's Literature Review* 84: 34–129.
　　Biographical sketch, discussion of literary career, excerpts from reviews and commentary.

Senick, Gerard J. "Philip Pullman." *Authors and Artists for Young Adults* 41: 133–42.
   Biographical sketch with portrait, discussion of major works.

ARTHUR RANSOME, 1884–1967

Web Sites

"Arthur Ransome." *BBC Books*. Last accessed 11 Dec. 2003. http://www.bbc.co .uk/arts/books/author/ransome/.
   Biographical sketch; discussion of major works.

"Arthur Ransome." *CORAL (Caribbean Online Resource and Archive)*. 2002. Last accessed 22 Dec. 2003. http://www.caribbeanedu.com/coral/refcen/ Biography/readbio.asp?id=196.
   Biographical sketch.

The Arthur Ransome Site. 27 May 2003. Last accessed 11 Dec. 2003. http:// www.arthur-ransome.org/ar/.
   Extensive site. Includes information on Ransome's life and books.

Biographies and Criticism

"Arthur (Michell) Ransome." *Children's Literature Review* 8: 141–84.
   Biographical sketch, discussion of literary career, excerpts from reviews and commentary.

Curtis, Donnelyn. "Ransome, Arthur." Silvey, *The Essential Guide to Children's Books and Their Creators*. 375–76.
   Biographical sketch.

Lynch, Catherine M. "Arthur Ransome." Hettinga and Schmidt, *British Children's Writers, 1914–1960* (*Dictionary of Literary Biography* 160): 217–27.
   Discussion of literary career and influence.

"Ransome, Arthur (Michell)." *Something About the Author* 22: 198–205.
   Biographical sketch with portrait, discussion of major works.

Bibliographies

"Ransome, Arthur." Hendrickson, *Children's Literature: A Guide to the Criticism*. 223–24.
   Lists books and articles about Ransome and his works.

CHRIS RASCHKA, 1959–

Web Sites

Wilson, Etta. "Chris Raschka and his Round-the-World Sardine 'Arlene.'" *BookPage*. 1998. Last accessed 11 Dec. 2003. http://www.bookpage.com/9809bp/chris_raschka.html.
Interview with Raschka.

Biographies and Criticism

Aycock, Edward M. "Raschka, Chris." Silvey, *The Essential Guide to Children's Books and Their Creators*. 376–77.
Biographical sketch.

"Raschka, Christopher (Chris Raschka)." *Something About the Author* 117: 150–56.
Biographical sketch with portrait, discussion of major works.

ELLEN RASKIN, 1928–1984

Web Sites

Kruse, Ginny Moore."Ellen Raskin: Notable Wisconsin Author." *Wisconsin Authors and Illustrators (University of Wisconsin)*. 2000. Last accessed 11 Dec. 2003. http://www.education.wisc.edu/ccbc/wisauth/raskin/main.htm.
Biographical sketch. Includes links to information about Raskin's "Westing Game Manuscript" and an audio file of her discussion of it.

Biographies and Criticism

Amster, Mara Ilyse. "Raskin, Ellen." Silvey, *The Essential Guide to Children's Books and Their Creators*. 376–78.
Biographical sketch.

"Ellen Raskin." *Children's Literature Review* 12: 213–29.
Biographical sketch, discussion of literary career, excerpts from reviews and commentary.

Karrenbrock, Marilyn H. "Ellen Raskin." Estes, *American Writers for Children Since 1960: Fiction (Dictionary of Literary Biography* 52): 314–25.
Discussion of literary career and influence.

Olson, Marilynn Strasser. *Ellen Raskin*. Boston: Twayne Publishers, 1991.
Critical commentary on Raskin's works.

"Raskin, Ellen." *Something About the Author* 139: 188–94.
Biographical sketch with portrait, discussion of major works.

MARJORIE KINNAN RAWLINGS, 1896–1953

Web Sites

Fernandez, Kay Harwell. "Marjorie Kinnan Rawlings at Cross Creek." *Literary Traveler*. 2003. Last accessed 11 Dec. 2003. http://www.literarytraveler .com/rawlings/rawlings.htm.
Biographical sketch.

The Marjorie Kinnan Rawlings Society. 2003. Last accessed 11 Dec. 2003. http://web.english.ufl.edu/rawlings/.
Includes biographical information about Rawlings.

Biographies and Criticism

Kilgo, Reese Danley. "Marjorie Kinnan Rawlings." Cech, *American Writers for Children, 1900–1960* (*Dictionary of Literary Biography* 22): 282–85.
Discussion of literary career and influence.

"Marjorie Kinnan Rawlings." *Children's Literature Review* 63: 115–37.
Biographical sketch, discussion of literary career, excerpts from reviews and commentary.

"Rawlings, Marjorie Kinnan." *Something About the Author* 100: 205–8.
Biographical sketch with portrait, discussion of major works.

Sieruta, Peter D. "Rawlings, Marjorie Kinnan." Silvey, *The Essential Guide to Children's Books and Their Creators*. 378–79.
Biographical sketch.

H. A. REY, 1898–1977, AND MARGRET REY, 1906–1996

Web Sites

"Curious George." *Houghton Mifflin*. 2003. Last accessed 27 Dec. 2003. http://www.houghtonmifflinbooks.com/features/cgsite/.
Publisher web site. Includes biographical information about the Reys.

"H. A. and Margret Rey Collection." *de Grummond Collection*. 21 Jan. 2003. Last accessed 11 Dec. 2003. http://www.lib.usm.edu/~degrum/html/collectionhl/ ch-reys.shtml.
Biographical sketch, link to a viritual exhibit on the Reys.

"H. A. Rey." *Kidsreads.com*. 2003. Last accessed 11 Dec. 2003. http://www.kids reads.com/authors/au-rey-ha.asp.
Biographical sketch.

"Margret Rey." *Kidsreads.com*. 2003. Last accessed 11 Dec. 2003. http://www .kidsreads.com/authors/au-rey-margret.asp.
Biographical sketch.

Biographies and Criticism

"H(ans) A(ugusto) Rey 1898–1977 Margret Rey 1906–   ." *Children's Literature Review* 5: 188–200.
Biographical sketch, discussion of literary career, excerpts from reviews and commentary.

Horton, Nancy. "Rey, H(ans) A(ugusto)." Cullinan and Person, *The Continuum Encyclopedia of Children's Literature*. 667–68.
Biographical sketch.

Jones, J. Sydney. "Rey, Margret (Elizabeth)." *Something About the Author*. 86: 193–98.
Biographical sketch with portrait, discussion of major works.

"Rey, H(ans) A(ugusto)." *Something About the Author* 100: 208–12.
Biographical sketch with portrait, discussion of major works.

Smith, Louisa. "H. A. Rey." Cech, *American Writers for Children, 1900–1960* (*Dictionary of Literary Biography* 22): 286–89.
Discussion of literary career and influence.

CHRISTINA GEORGINA ROSSETTI, 1830–1894

Web Sites

"Christina Rossetti." *Academy of American Poets*. 2003. Last accessed 11 Dec. 2003. http://www.poets.org/poets/poets.cfm?prmID=733.
Biographical sketch, selected bibliography, links to related sites.

"Christina Rossetti." *The Victorian Web*. Last accessed 11 Dec. 2003. http://www.victorianweb.org/authors/crossetti/crov.html.
Extensive site with numerous biographical and critical resources.

Liukkonen, Petri. "Christina Rossetti." *Author's Calendar*. Ed. Ari Pesonen. 2000. Last accessed 11 Dec. 2003. http://www.kirjasto.sci.fi/rossetti.htm.
Biographical sketch and discussion of Rossetti's major works.

Biographies and Criticism

"Christina Rossetti." *Authors and Artists for Young Adults* 51: 169–77.
Biographical sketch with portrait, discussion of major works.

Deifendeifer, Anne E. "Rossetti, Christina." Silvey, *Children's Books and Their Creators*. 563–64.
Biographical sketch.

Susina, Jan. "Christina Georgina Rossetti." Khorana, *British Children's Writers, 1800–1880* (*Dictionary of Literary Biography* 163): 239–46.
Discussion of literary career and influence.

Bibliographies

Crump, Rebecca W. *Christina Rossetti: A Reference Guide*. Boston: G. K. Hall, 1976.
Describes works by and about Rossetti.

J. K. ROWLING, 1965–

Web Sites

"Harry Potter." *Scholastic*. 2003. Last accessed 12 Dec. 2003. http://www .scholastic.com/harrypotter/books/.
Publisher web site for Rowling's Harry Potter books. Includes a biographical sketch on Rowling.

"J. K. Rowling." *BBC Books*. Last accessed 12 Dec. 2003. http://www.bbc.co .uk/arts/books/author/rowling/.
Biographical sketch.

J. K. Rowling Official Site. 2004. Last accessed 19 July 2004. www.jkrowling .com.
Author site. Includes biographical information.

"Kidsread.com Presents Harry Potter." *Kidsread.com*. Last accessed 12 Dec. 2003. http://www.kidsreads.com/HarryPotter/.
Includes biographical sketch, interview with Rowling.

Stephenson, Sarah Kate. "The Real Magic of Harry Potter." *The Looking Glass* 4: 2 (2 Aug. 2000). Last accessed 12 Dec. 2003. http://www.the-looking-glass.net/rabbit/4.2/academy.html.
Critical essay.

Biographies and Criticism

"J. K. Rowling." *Children's Literature Review* 80: 174–215.
Biographical sketch, discussion of literary career, excerpts from reviews and commentary.

"J. K. Rowling." *Contemporary Literary Criticism* 137: 304–41.
Discussion of literary career, excerpts from reviews and commentary.

Jones, J. Sydney. "Rowling, J(oanne) K." *Something About the Author* 109: 199–202.
Biographical sketch with portrait, discussion of major works.

Loer, Stephanie. "Rowling, J. K." Silvey, *The Essential Guide to Children's Books and Their Creators*. 388–89.
Biographical sketch.

ANTOINE DE SAINT-EXUPÉRY, 1900–1944

Web Sites

Liukkonen, Petri. "Antoine de Saint-Exupéry." *Author's Calendar*. Ed. Ari Pesonen. 2000. Last accessed 12 Dec. 2003. http://www.kirjasto.sci.fi/exupery.htm.
Biographical sketch and discussion of de Saint-Exupéry's major works.

Biographies and Criticism

"Antoine (Jean Baptiste Marie Roger) de Saint-Exupéry." *Children's Literature Review* 10: 137–61.
Biographical sketch, discussion of literary career, excerpts from reviews and commentary.

"Saint-Exupéry, Antoine de." *Something About the Author* 20: 154–63.
Biographical sketch with portrait, discussion of major works.

Sieruta, Peter D. "Saint-Exupéry, Antoine de." Silvey, *Children's Books and Their Creators*. 569–70.
Biographical sketch.

RICHARD SCARRY, 1919–1994

Web Sites

Liukkonen, Petri. "Richard Scarry." *Author's Calendar*. Ed. Ari Pesonen. 2000. Last accessed 12 Dec. 2003. http://www.kirjasto.sci.fi/rscarry.htm.
Biographical sketch and discussion of Scarry's major works.

"Richard Scarry Papers." *de Grummond Collection*. 7 July 2001. Last accessed 12 Dec. 2003. http://www.lib.usm.edu/%7Edegrum/html/research/findaids/scarry.htm.
Description of Richard Scarry archival papers at the de Grummond Collection. Includes biographical sketch, discussion of major works.

Biographies and Criticism

Brabander, Jennifer M. "Scarry, Richard." Silvey, *The Essential Guide to Children's Books and Their Creators*. 395–96.
Biographical sketch.

Lemont, Bobbie Burch. "Richard Scarry." Estes, *American Writers for Children Since 1960: Poets, Illustrators, and Nonfiction Authors* (*Dictionary of Literary Biography* 61): 248–57.
Discussion of literary career and influence.

"Richard Scarry." *Children's Literature Review* 41: 145–72.
Biographical sketch, discussion of literary career, excerpts from reviews and commentary.

"Scarry, Richard (McClure)." *Something About the Author* 75: 163–70.
    Biographical sketch with portrait, discussion of major works.

JON SCIESZKA, 1954–

Web Sites

Colhoun, Ace. "The Stinky Interview." *The Peak, Simon Fraser University's Student Newspaper Since 1965* 92: 10 (11 Mar. 1996). Last accessed 12 Dec. 2003. http://www.peak.sfu.ca/the-peak/96-1/issue10/stinky.html.
    Interview with Scieszka.

"Jon Scieszka." *Kidsreads.com.* 2003. Last accessed 12 Dec. 2003. http://www.kidsreads.com/authors/au-scieszka-jon.asp.
    Autobiographical sketch, including instructions on the correct pronunciation of "Scieszka."

"Jon Scieszka." *Penguin Group (USA).* 2000. Last accessed 12 Dec. 2003. http://www.penguinputnam.com/Author/AuthorFrame?0000023137.
    Portrait and biographical sketch on publisher site.

Biographies and Criticism

Heppermann, Christine M. "Scieszka, Jon." Silvey, *The Essential Guide to Children's Books and Their Creators.* 401–2.
    Biographical sketch.

"Jon Scieszka." *Children's Literature Review* 27: 152–57.
    Biographical sketch, discussion of literary career, excerpts from reviews and commentary.

Shepherd, Ken. "Scieszka, Jon." *Authors and Artists for Young Adults* 21: 185–91.
    Biographical sketch with portrait, discussion of major works.

MAURICE SENDAK, 1928–

Web Sites

Gregory, Carol, and Inez Ramsey. "Maurice Sendak." *Kidsread.com.* 2003. Last accessed 12 Dec. 2003. http://www.kidsreads.com/authors/au-sendak-maurice.asp.
    Biographical sketch.

"Interview with Maurice Sendak." *Backstage\Lincoln Center (PBS).* Last accessed 12 Dec. 2003. http://www.pbs.org/lflc/dec17/sendak.htm.
    Short interview that focuses on his set design work.

"Maurice Sendak." *American Masters (PBS).* Last accessed 12 Dec. 2003. http://www.pbs.org/wnet/americanmasters/database/sendak_m.html.
    Biographical sketch.

"Maurice Sendak." *Steven Barclay Agency*. 2003. Last accessed 12 Dec. 2003. http://www.barclayagency.com/sendak.html.
  Sendak's literary agency page. Includes brief biography, list of major works, portrait of Sendak, and some of Sendak's illustrations and book jackets.

Biographies and Criticism

Cech, John. *Angels and Wild Things: The Archetypal Poetics of Maurice Sendak*. University Park: Pennsylvania State University Press, 1995.
  Book-length study on Sendak and his literary career.

Cotham, John. "Maurice Sendak." Estes, *American Writers for Children Since 1960: Poets, Illustrators, and Nonfiction Authors* (*Dictionary of Literary Biography* 61). 258–72.
  Discussion of literary career and influence.

Jones, J. Sydney. "Sendak, Maurice (Bernard)." *Something About the Author* 113: 160–70.
  Biographical sketch with portrait, discussion of major works.

Lanes, Selma G. *The Art of Maurice Sendak*. New York: Harry N. Abrams, 1980.
  Book-length study on Sendak and his works.

"Maurice Sendak." *Children's Literature Review* 74: 12–185.
  Biographical sketch, discussion of literary career, excerpts from reviews and commentary.

Russell, David L. "Sendak, Maurice (Bernard)." Cullinan and Person, *The Continuum Encyclopedia of Children's Literature*. 703–6.
  Biographical sketch.

Bibliographies

"Maurice Sendak." Rahn, *Children's Literature: An Annotated Bibliography of the History and Criticism*. 327–31.
  Lists books and articles about Sendak and his works.

"Sendak, Maurice B." Hendrickson, *Children's Literature: A Guide to the Criticism*. 237–43.
  List of books and articles about Sendak and his works.

KATE SEREDY, 1899–1975

Web Sites

"Kate Seredy Papers." *de Grummond Collection*. July 2001. Last accessed 12 Dec. 2003. http://www.lib.usm.edu/~degrum/html/research/findaids/seredy.htm.
  Description of Kate Seredy archival papers at the de Grummond Collection. Includes biographical sketch, discussion of major works.

Biographies and Criticism

"Kate Seredy." *Children's Literature Review* 10: 162–82.
Biographical sketch, discussion of literary career, excerpts from reviews and commentary.

Piehl, Kathy. "Kate Seredy." Cech, *American Writers for Children, 1900–1960 (Dictionary of Literary Biography* 22): 299–306.
Discussion of literary career and influence.

"Seredy, Kate." *Something About the Author* 1: 193.
Biographical sketch with portrait, discussion of major works.

Sieruta, Peter D. "Seredy, Kate." Silvey, *Children's Books and Their Creators.* 588–89.
Biographical sketch.

DR. SEUSS. *SEE* THEODOR SEUSS GEISEL

ANNA SEWELL, 1820–1878

Web Sites

"Anna Sewell." *CORAL (Caribbean Online Resource and Archive).* 2002. Last accessed 22 Dec. 2003. http://www.caribbeanedu.com/coral/refcen/Biography/readbio.asp?id=215.
Biographical sketch.

"Anna Sewell." *Dorling Kindersley Limited.* Last accessed 12 Dec. 2003. http://uk.dk.com/Author/AuthorFrame/0,1020,,00.html?id=1000029307.
Biographical sketch on publisher web site.

Longshaw, Jennifer. "Gentle Heart: The Story of Anna Sewell." *Nature of Animals.* 2001. Last accessed 12 Dec. 2003. http://www.natureofanimals.com/article1005.html.
Biographial sketch.

Project Gutenberg. 25 Dec. 2003. Last accessed 27 Dec. 2003. http://www.gutenberg.net/index.shtml.
Includes uncopyrighted online text for Sewell's *Black Beauty* (use the "Find an Ebook" link to find it).

Biographies and Criticism

"Anna Sewell." *Children's Literature Review* 17: 130–47.
Biographical sketch, discussion of literary career, excerpts from reviews and commentary.

Heppermann, Christine M. "Sewell, Anna." Silvey, *Children's Books and Their Creators.* 593–94.
Biographical sketch.

Prusty, Lopa. "Anna Sewell." Khorana, *British Children's Writers, 1800–1880* (*Dictionary of Literary Biography* 163): 259–66.
Discussion of literary career and influence.

"Sewell, Anna." *Something About the Author* 100: 213–15.
Biographical sketch with portrait, discussion of major works.

SHEL SILVERSTEIN, 1932–1999

Web Sites

Bruns, Ann L. "Shel Silverstein." *Kidsreads.com*. 2003. Last accessed 12 Dec. 2003. http://www.kidsreads.com/features/0204-silverstein-author.asp.
Photo, biographical sketch with links to information about his works.

"Shel Silverstein." *Academy of American Poets*. 12 Feb. 2001. Last accessed 12 Dec. 2003. http://www.poets.org/poets/poets.cfm?prmID=105.
Biographical sketch, selected bibliography, links to related sites.

"Shel Silverstein." *HarperChildrens.com*. Last accessed 12 Dec. 2003. http://www.harperchildrens.com/hch/author/features/silverstein.asp.
Publisher site. Biographical sketch.

Biographies and Criticism

Amster, Mara Ilyse. "Silverstein, Shel." Silvey, *The Essential Guide to Children's Books and Their Creators*. 413–14.
Biographical sketch.

"Shel Silverstein." *Children's Literature Review* 5: 208–13.
Biographical sketch, discussion of literary career, excerpts from reviews and commentary.

"Silverstein, Shel(by) (Uncle Shelby)." *Something About the Author* 92: 208–11.
Biographical sketch with portrait, discussion of major works.

ISAAC BASHEVIS SINGER, 1904–1991

Web Sites

"Isaac Bashevis Singer." *Fantastic Fiction*. 2003. Last accessed 12 Dec. 2003. http://www.fantasticfiction.co.uk/authors/Isaac_Bashevis_Singer.htm.
Lists Singer's major works.

"The Nobel Prize in Literature 1978: Isaac Bashevis Singer." *Nobel E-Museum*. 16 June 2000. http://www.nobel.se/literature/laureates/1978/index.html.
From the official web site of the Nobel Prize Foundation. Includes biographical profile and discussion of major literary works, portrait, text of Nobel Prize acceptance speech.

Biographies and Criticism

Iskander, Sylvia W. "Singer, Isaac Bashevis." Estes, *American Writers for Children Since 1960: Fiction (Dictionary of Literary Biography* 52): 334–52.
Discussion of literary career and influence.

Kvilhaug, Sarah Guille. "Singer, Isaac Bashevis." Silvey, *The Essential Guide to Children's Books and Their Creators*. 416–17.
Biographical sketch.

Rechtman, Elana. "Singer, Isaac Bashevis, (pseud. Warshofky)." Cullinan and Person, *The Continuum Encyclopedia of Children's Literature*. 722–23.
Biographical sketch.

"Singer, Isaac Bashevis." *Children's Literature Review* 1: 173–76.
Biographical sketch, discussion of literary career, excerpts from reviews and commentary.

Telgen, Diane. "Isaac Bashevis Singer." *Authors and Artists for Young Adults* 32: 137–54.
Biographical sketch with portrait, discussion of major works.

Bibliographies

"Singer, Isaac Bashevis." Hendrickson, *Children's Literature: A Guide to the Criticism*. 249–50.
Lists books and articles about Singer and his works.

WILLIAM SLEATOR, 1945–

Web Sites

"William Sleator." *Penguin Group (USA)*. 2000. Last accessed 12 Dec. 2003.
http://www.penguinputnam.com/Author/AuthorFrame?0000024064.
Publisher web site. Short biographical sketch.

"William Sleator Bibliography." *Fantastic Fiction*. 2003. Last accessed 12 Dec. 2003. http://www.fantasticfiction.co.uk/authors/William_Sleator.htm.
Lists Sleator's major works.

Williams, Royce. *The Green Futures of Tycho*. 29 Oct. 2003. Last accessed 12 Dec. 2003. http://www.tycho.org/.
Extensive site devoted to Sleator's *The Green Futures of Tycho*. Includes biographical material on Sleator.

Biographies and Criticism

Jones, J. Sydney. "William Sleator." *Authors and Artists for Young Adults* 39: 173–78.
Biographical sketch with portrait, discussion of major works.

Sieruta, Peter D. "Sleator, William." Silvey, *The Essential Guide to Children's Books and Their Creators*. 418–19.
Biographical sketch.

"William Sleator." *Children's Literature Review* 29: 196–208.
Biographical sketch, discussion of literary career, excerpts from reviews and commentary.

LEMONY SNICKET. *SEE* DANIEL HANDLER

ZILPHA KEATLEY SNYDER, 1927–

Web Sites

Zilpha Keatley Snyder. Last accessed 12 Dec. 2003. http://www.zksnyder.com/.
Author web site. Includes biographical material.

"Zilpha Keatley Snyder." *Fantastic Fiction*. 2003. Last accessed 12 Dec. 2003.
http://www.fantasticfiction.co.uk/authors/Zilpha_Keatley_Snyder.htm.
Lists Snyder's major works.

Biographies and Criticism

"Autobiography Feature: Zilpha Keatley Snyder." *Something About the Author* 112: 179–90.
Autobiographical sketch.

Jones, J. Sydney. "Snyder, Zilpha Keatley." *Something About the Author* 110: 205–10.
Biographical sketch with portrait, discussion of major works.

Sieruta, Peter D. "Snyder, Zilpha Keatley." Silvey, *The Essential Guide to Children's Books and Their Creators*. 423–24.
Biographical sketch.

"Zilpha Keatley Snyder." *Children's Literature Review* 31: 149–70.
Biographical sketch, discussion of literary career, excerpts from reviews and commentary.

GARY SOTO, 1952–

Web Sites

"Gary Soto." *Penguin Group (USA)*. 2000. Last accessed 12 Dec. 2003. http://www.penguinputnam.com/Author/AuthorFrame/?0000032854.
Biographical sketch.

The Official Gary Soto Website. Last accessed 12 Dec. 2003. http://www.garysoto.com/.
Author web site. Includes biographical information.

Reuben, Paul P. "Chapter 10: Late Twentieth Century—Gary Soto (1952–)."
    *PAL: Perspectives in American Literature—A Research and Reference
    Guide.* 10 Jan. 2003. Last accessed 12 Dec. 2003. http://www.csustan.edu/
    english/reuben/pal/chap10/soto.html.
    Includes primary and secondary bibliographies, portrait, links to related
sites.

Biographies and Criticism

Brabander, Jennifer M. "Soto, Gary." Silvey, *The Essential Guide to Children's
    Books and Their Creators.* 425–26.
    Biographical sketch.

"Gary Soto." *Children's Literature Review* 38: 183–207.
    Biographical sketch, discussion of literary career, excerpts from reviews
and commentary.

"Jones, J. Sydney." *Something About the Author* 120: 209–15.
    Biographical sketch with portrait, discussion of major works.

Torres, Héctor Avalos. "Gary Soto." Lomeli, Francisco A., and Carl R. Shirley,
    eds. *Chicano Writers, First Series* (*Dictionary of Literary Biography* 82):
    246–52. Detroit, MI: Gale, 1989.
    Discussion of literary career and influence.

ELIZABETH GEORGE SPEARE, 1908–1994

Web Sites

"Speare, Elizabeth George." *Educational Paperback Association.* Last accessed
    12 Dec. 2003. http://www.edupaperback.org/showauth.cfm?authid=85.
    Biographical sketch, discussion of her works.

Biographies and Criticism

Apseloff, Marilyn. *Elizabeth George Speare.* New York: Twayne Publishers,
    1991.
    Critical commentary on Speare's works.

"Elizabeth George Speare." *Children's Literature Review* 8: 204–11.
    Biographical sketch, discussion of literary career, excerpts from reviews
and commentary.

Kantar, Andrew. "Speare, Elizabeth George." Cullinan and Person, *The Contin-
    uum Encyclopedia of Children's Literature.* 738–40.
    Biographical sketch.

"Speare, Elizabeth George." *Something About the Author* 62: 163–69.
    Biographical sketch with portrait, discussion of major works.

JERRY SPINELLI, 1941–

Web Sites

"Jerry Spinelli." *Kidsreads.com*. 2003. Last accessed 12 Dec. 2003. http://www
.kidsreads.com/authors/au-spinelli-jerry.asp.
Autobiographical statement.

"Jerry Spinelli." *Random House*. 2003. Last accessed 12 Dec. 2003. http://www
.randomhouse.com/features/jerryspinelli/.
Publisher web site. Includes biographical information.

Kerby, Mona. "Jerry Spinelli." *The Author Corner*. 19 Apr. 2000. Last accessed
12 Dec. 2003. http://www.carr.lib.md.us/authco/spinelli-j.htm.
Short biographical sketch, portrait, interview with Spinelli.

"Spinelli, Jerry." *Educational Paperback Association*. Last accessed 12 Dec.
2003. http://www.edupaperback.org/showauth.cfm?authid=74.
Biographical sketch with list of major works.

Biographies and Criticism

Broughton, Mary Ariail. "Spinelli, Jerry." Cullinan and Person, *The Continuum
Encyclopedia of Children's Literature*. 741–42.
Biographical sketch.

"Jerry Spinelli." *Children's Literature Review* 82: 161–80.
Biographical sketch, discussion of literary career, excerpts from reviews
and commentary.

Jones, J. Sydney. "Spinelli, Jerry." *Authors and Artists for Young Adults* 41: 163–69.
Biographical sketch with portrait, discussion of major works.

JOHANNA SPYRI, 1827–1901

Web Sites

Bailey, Suzanne. *The Heidi by Johanna Spyri Website*. 2003. Last accessed 12
Dec. 2003. http://www.geocities.com/EnchantedForest/Glade/8905/.
Extensive web site with biographical information about Spryi and links to
further online resources.

Project Gutenberg. 25 Dec. 2003. Last accessed 27 Dec. 2003. http://www
.gutenberg.net/index.shtml.
Includes uncopyrighted online texts for several of Spyri's works, including
Heidi (use the "Find an Ebook" link to find texts by Spyri).

Biographies and Criticism

Heppermann, Christine. "Spyri, Johanna." Silvey, *Children's Books and Their
Creators*. 623.
Biographical sketch.

"Johanna (Heusser) Spyri." *Children's Literature Review* 13: 174–86.
Biographical sketch, discussion of literary career, excerpts from reviews and commentary.

"Spyri, Johanna (Heusser)." *Something About the Author* 100: 221–24.
Biographical sketch with portrait, discussion of major works.

WILLIAM STEIG, 1907–2003

Web Sites

Hawtree, Christopher. "Obituary: William Steig." *The Guardian.* 7 Oct. 2003. Last accessed 12 Dec. 2003. http://www.guardian.co.uk/obituaries/story/0,3604,1057343,00.html.
Biographical sketch.

William Steig. 2003. Last accessed 12 Dec. 2003. http://www.williamsteig.com/.
Late author web site (appears to be sponsored by the publisher Farrar, Straus, and Giroux). Includes biographical information.

"William Steig." *Kidsreads.com.* 2003. Last accessed 12 Dec. 2003. http://www.kidsreads.com/authors/au-steig-william.asp.
Biographical sketch.

Biographies and Criticism

Anderson, Joy. "William Steig." Estes, *American Writers for Children Since 1960: Poets, Illustrators, and Nonfiction Authors* (*Dictionary of Literary Biography* 61): 297–305.
Discussion of literary career and influence.

Jones, J. Sydney. "Steig, William." *Something About the Author* 111: 170–77.
Biographical sketch with portrait, discussion of major works.

Robinson, Lolly. "Steig, William." Silvey, *The Essential Guide to Children's Books and Their Creators.* 433–34.
Biographical sketch.

"William Steig." *Children's Literature Review* 15: 175–202.
Biographical sketch, discussion of literary career, excerpts from reviews and commentary.

ROBERT LOUIS STEVENSON, 1850–1894

Web Sites

Booth, Thomas H. "Robert Louis Stevenson and Western Samoa." *Literary Traveler.* 2003. Last accessed 12 Dec. 2003. http://www.literarytraveler.com/robertlouisstevenson/stevenson.htm.
Biographical sketch.

Liukkonen, Petri. "Robert Louis Stevenson." *Author's Calendar*. Ed. Ari Pesonen. 2000. Last accessed 12 Dec. 2003. http://www.kirjasto.sci.fi/rlsteven.htm. Biographical sketch and discussion of Stevenson's major works.

Project Gutenberg. 25 Dec. 2003. Last accessed 27 Dec. 2003. http://www .gutenberg.net/index.shtml.
Includes uncopyrighted online texts for several of Stevenson's works, including *A Child's Garden of Verse* (use the "Find an Ebook" link to find texts by Stevenson).

"Robert Louis Stevenson." *CORAL (Caribbean Online Resource and Archive)*. 2002. Last accessed 22 Dec. 2003. http://www.caribbeanedu.com/coral/ refcen/Biography/readbio.asp?id=228.
Biographical sketch.

The Robert Louis Stevenson Web Site. Ed. Richard Dury. Last accessed 22 Dec. 2003. http://wwwesterni.unibg.it/rls/rls.htm.
Extensive web site including information on various aspects of Stevenson and his works, as well as links to related sites.

Biographies and Criticism

Chlebek, Diana A. "Robert Louis Stevenson." Zaidman, *British Children's Writers, 1880–1914* (*Dictionary of Literary Biography* 141): 271–83.
Discussion of literary career and influence.

Kvilhaug, Sarah Guille. "Stevenson, Robert Louis." Silvey, *Children's Books and Their Creators*. 630–31.
Biographical sketch.

"Robert Louis (Balfour) Stevenson." *Children's Literature Review* 10: 193–235.
Biographical sketch, discussion of literary career, excerpts from reviews and commentary on Stevenson's *Treasure Island*.

"Robert Louis (Balfour) Stevenson." *Children's Literature Review* 11: 222–43.
Biographical sketch, discussion of literary career, excerpts from reviews and commentary on Stevenson's *A Child's Garden of Verses*.

"Stevenson, Robert Louis (Balfour)." *Something About the Author* 100: 225–30.
Biographical sketch with portrait, discussion of major works.

R. L. STINE, 1943–

Web Sites

"R. L. Stine." *Kidsreads.com*. 2003. Last accessed 12 Dec. 2003. http://www .kidsreads.com/series/series-nightmare-author.asp.
Portrait, biographical sketch, interview.

"R. L. Stine." *Scholastic*. 2003. Last accessed 12 Dec. 2003. http://www.scholastic .com/goosebumps/books/stine/index.htm.
Publisher web site. Includes biographical information.

"R. L. Stine (Robert Lawrence Stine) Bibliography." *Fantastic Fiction*. 2003. Last accessed 12 Dec. 2003. http://www.fantasticfiction.co.uk/authors/R_L_Stine.htm.
Lists Stine's major works.

Biographies and Criticism

"R. L. Stine." *Children's Literature Review* 37: 101–23.
Biographical sketch, discussion of literary career, excerpts from reviews and commentary.

Small, Dede. "Stine, R(obert) L(awrence)." Cullinan and Person, *The Continuum Encyclopedia of Children's Literature*. 752–53.
Biographical sketch.

"Stine, R(obert) L(awrence)." *Something About the Author* 129: 177–85.
Biographical sketch with portrait, discussion of major works.

EDWARD L. STRATEMEYER, 1862–1930

Web Sites

Keeline, James D. "Stratemeyer Syndicate." *Keeline.com*. Last accessed 27 Dec. 2003. http://keeline.com/StratemeyerSyndicate.html.
Includes a biographical sketch about Stratemeyer, and information about the Stratemeyer Syndicate and the series it produced.

Project Gutenberg. 25 Dec. 2003. Last accessed 27 Dec. 2003. http://www.gutenberg.net/index.shtml.
Includes uncopyrighted online texts for several of Stratemeyer's works, including *The Rover Boys at College* (use the "Find an Ebook" link to find texts by Stratemeyer or pen names used by his Stratemeyer Syndicate).

Biographies and Criticism

Billman, Carol. *The Secret of the Stratemeyer Syndicate: Nancy Drew, the Hardy Boys, and the Million Dollar Fiction Factory*. New York: Ungar, 1986.
Book-length study of the Stratemeyer Syndicate and its influence on children's and young adult literature.

Cullinan, Bernice E. "Stratemeyer, Edward." Cullinan and Person, *The Continuum Encyclopedia of Children's Literature*. 760–61.
Biographical sketch.

Johnson, Deidre. *Edward Stratemeyer and the Stratemeyer Syndicate*. New York: Twayne Publishers, 1993.
Book-length study on Stratemeyer and his literary influence.

"Stratemeyer, Edward L." *Something About the Author* 100: 230–38.
Biographical sketch with portrait, discussion of major works.

Taylor, Mary-Agnes. "Edward Stratemeyer." Estes, *American Writers for Children Before 1900* (*Dictionary of Literary Biography* 42): 351–62.
Discussion of literary career and influence.

Bibliographies

"Stratemeyer, Edward." Hendrickson, *Children's Literature: A Guide to the Criticism.* 261–62.
Lists books and articles about Stratemeyer and his works.

MILDRED D. TAYLOR, 1943–

Web Sites

Crowe, Chris. "Mildred D. Taylor." *Mississippi Writers Page.* 28 Apr. 2003. Last accessed 13 Dec. 2003. http://www.olemiss.edu/mwp/dir/taylor_mildred/index.html.
Biographical sketch; links to other online resources.

Libhardt, Melissa, Kimberly Martin, and Katie Schwegel. "Mildred Taylor." *Voices from the Gaps: Women Writers of Color.* 1 Dec. 2000. Last accessed 13 Dec. 2003. http://voices.cla.umn.edu/authors/TAYLORmildred.html.
Biographical sketch, discussion of Taylor's major works.

"Mildred Taylor." *CORAL (Caribbean Online Resource and Archive).* 2002. Last accessed 22 Dec. 2003. http://www.caribbeanedu.com/coral/refcen/Biography/readbio.asp?id=238.
Biographical sketch.

"Mildred Taylor." *Penguin Group (USA).* 2000. Last accessed 13 Dec. 2003. http://www.penguinputnam.com/Author/AuthorFrame?0000025506.
Biographical sketch from publisher web site.

"Taylor, Mildred." *Educational Paperback Association.* Last accessed 13 Dec. 2003. http://www.edupaperback.org/showauth.cfm?authid=75.
Biographical sketch with selected list of major works.

Biographies and Criticism

Holtze, Sally Holmes. "Taylor, Mildred." Silvey, *The Essential Guide to Children's Books and Their Creators.* 441–42.
Biographical sketch.

"Mildred D. Taylor." *Children's Literature Review* 90: 119–49.
Biographical sketch, discussion of literary career, excerpts from reviews and commentary.

"Taylor, Mildred." *Something About the Author* 135: 205–9.
Biographical sketch with portrait, discussion of major works.

Wright, David A. "Mildred D. Taylor." Estes, *American Writers for Children Since 1960: Fiction* (*Dictionary of Literary Biography* 52): 364–68.
Discussion of literary career and influence.

JAMES THURBER, 1894–1961

Web Sites

"James Thurber Bibliography." *Fantastic Fiction.* 2003. Last accessed 13 Dec. 2003. http://www.fantasticfiction.co.uk/authors/James_Thurber.htm.
Lists Thurber's major works.

"James Thurber: We Call Him Jamie." *James Thurber House.* Last accessed 13 Dec. 2003. http://www.thurberhouse.org/DefaultJamesThurber.htm.
Biographical sketch.

Liukkonen, Petri. "James Thurber." *Author's Calendar.* Ed. Ari Pesonen. 2000. Last accessed 13 Dec. 2003. http://www.kirjasto.sci.fi/thurber.htm.
Biographical sketch and discussion of Thurber's major works.

Biographies and Criticism

Kvilhaug, Sarah Guille. "Thurber, James." Silvey, *The Essential Guide to Children's Books and Their Creators.* 447–48.
Biographical sketch.

"Thurber, James (Grover)." *Something About the Author* 13: 235–57.
Biographical sketch with portrait, discussion of major works.

Vousden, E. Charles. "James Thurber." Cech, *American Writers for Children, 1900–1960* (*Dictionary of Literary Biography* 22): 315–20.
Discussion of literary career and influence.

Bibliographies

"Thurber, James (George)." Lynn, *Fantasy Literature for Children and Young Adults.* 875.
Lists Thurber's major works.

J.R.R. TOLKIEN, 1892–1973

Web Sites

The Barrow-Downs. Last accessed 13 Dec. 2003. http://www.barrowdowns.com/Welcome.asp.
Extensive site. Includes *The Middle-Earth Encyclopedia.*

"J.R.R. Tolkien." *BBC Books.* Last accessed 13 Dec. 2003. http://www.bbc.co.uk/arts/books/author/tolkien/.
Portrait, biographical sketch, discussion of major works, links to other sites of interest.

Liukkonen, Petri. "John Ronald Reuel Tolkien." *Author's Calendar*. Ed. Ari Pesonen. 2000. Last accessed 13 Dec. 2003. http://www.kirjasto.sci.fi/tolkien .htm.
Biographical sketch and discussion of Tolkien's major works.

The Tolkien Society Home Page. 2003. Last accessed 13 Dec. 2003. http://www .tolkiensociety.org/index.html.
Extensive site. Includes biographical information.

Biographies and Criticism

Duriez, Colin. "J.R.R. Tolkien." Hettinga and Schmidt, *British Children's Writers, 1914–1960* (*Dictionary of Literary Biography* 160): 254–71.
Discussion of literary career and influence.

George, Michael W. "J.R.R. Tolkien." Harris-Fain, *British Fantasy and Science-Fiction Writers, 1918–1960* (*Dictionary of Literary Biography* 255): 237–50.
Discussion of literary career and influence.

Hoke, Elizabeth C. "Tolkien, J.R.R." Silvey, *The Essential Guide to Children's Books and Their Creators*. 448–49.
Biographical sketch.

"J(ohn) R(onald) R(euel) Tolkien." *Children's Literature Review* 56: 149–81.
Biographical sketch, discussion of literary career, excerpts from reviews and commentary.

"Tolkien, J(ohn) R(onald) R(euel)." *Something About the Author* 100: 239–44.
Biographical sketch with portrait, discussion of major works.

White, Michael. *Tolkien: A Biography*. London: Little, Brown, 2001.
Book-length study of Tolkien and his literary career.

Bibliographies

"John Ronald Reuel Tolkien." Rahn, *Children's Literature: An Annotated Bibliography of the History and Criticism*. 354–58.
Lists books and articles about Tolkien and his works.

"Tolkien, J(ohn) R(euel)." Lynn, *Fantasy Literature for Children and Young Adults*. 876–91.
Lists books and articles about Tolkien and his works.

SUE TOWNSEND, 1946–

Web Sites

"Sue Townsend." *BBC Books*. Last accessed 13 Dec. 2003. http://www.bbc.co.uk/ arts/books/author/townsend/index.shtml.
Biographical sketch.

"Sue Townsend." *CORAL (Caribbean Online Resource and Archive)*. 2002. Last accessed 22 Dec. 2003. http://www.caribbeanedu.com/coral/refcen/Biography/readbio.asp?id=243.
Biographical sketch.

Biographies and Criticism

Gillis, Mary. "Sue Townsend." *Authors and Artists for Young Adults* 28: 191–96.
Biographical sketch with portrait, discussion of major works.

Tibbles, Sue. *"Secret Diary of Adrian Mole."* Watson, *The Cambridge Guide to Children's Literature in English*. Cambridge: Cambridge University Press, 2001. 638.
Discusses Townsend's *Secret Diary of Adrian Mole*.

P. L. TRAVERS, 1899–1996

Web Sites

Anemaat, Louise. "Guide to the Papers of P. L. Travers." *State Library of New South Wales*. 1991. Last accessed 28 Dec. 2003. http://www.sl.nsw.gov.au/mssguide/ptravers.pdf.
Description of P. L. Travers archival papers at the State Library of New South Wales. Includes biographical sketch, discussion of major works. PDF file.

"P. L. Travers Bibliography." *Fantastic Fiction*. 2003. Last accessed 13 Dec. 2003. http://www.fantasticfiction.co.uk/authors/P_L_Travers.htm.
Lists Travers's major works.

Biographies and Criticism

Pilgrim, Jodi. "Travers, P(amela) L(yndon)." Cullinan and Person, *The Continuum Encyclopedia of Children's Literature*. 783–84.
Biographical sketch.

"Travers, P(amela) L(yndon)." *Children's Literature Review* 2: 175–79.
Biographical sketch, discussion of literary career, excerpts from reviews and commentary.

"Travers, P(amela) L(yndon)." *Something About the Author* 100: 244–47.
Biographical sketch with portrait, discussion of major works.

Bibliographies

"Travers, P(amela) L." Hendrickson, *Children's Literature: A Guide to the Criticism*. 272–74.
Lists books and articles about Travers and her works.

MARK TWAIN. *SEE* SAMUEL LANGHORNE CLEMENS

UNCLE REMUS. *SEE* JOEL CHANDLER HARRIS

CHRIS VAN ALLSBURG, 1949–

Web Sites

"Author Profile: Chris Van Allsburg." *Houghton Mifflin*. 2003. Last accessed 13 Dec. 2003. http://www.eduplace.com/author/vanallsburg/.
   Publisher web site. Includes biographical sketch, and an interview by Stephanie Loer.

Canow, Joanne. "Surrealism and Dream: Chris Van Allsburg's Picturebooks." *The Looking Glass* 7: 3 (2 Sept. 2003). Last accessed 13 Dec. 2003. http://www.the-looking-glass.net/v7i3/picture.html.
   Critical essay.

"Chris Van Allsburg." *KidsReads.com*. 2003. Last accessed 27 Dec. 2003. http://www.kidsreads.com/authors/au-van-allsburg-chris.asp.
   Biographical sketch.

"The World of Chris Van Allsburg." *Houghton Mifflin*. 2003. Last accessed 27 Dec. 2003. http://www.houghtonmifflinbooks.com/authors/vanallsburg/author.shtml.
   Publisher web site. Biographical sketch; text of acceptance speeches for the 1982 and 1986 Caldecott Medals.

Biographies and Criticism

Ingram, Laura. "Chris Van Allsburg." Estes, *American Writers for Children Since 1960: Poets, Illustrators, and Nonfiction Writers* (*Dictionary of Literary Biography* 52). 306–13.
   Discussion of literary career and influence.

Jones, J. Sydney. "Van Allsburg, Chris." *Something About the Author* 105: 213–19.
   Biographical sketch with portrait, discussion of major works.

Loer, Stephanie. "Van Allsburg, Chris." Silvey, *The Essential Guide to Children's Books and Their Creators*. 455–57.
   Biographical sketch.

"Van Allsburg, Chris." *Children's Literature Review* 13: 204–14.
   Biographical sketch, discussion of literary career, excerpts from reviews and commentary.

JULES VERNE, 1828–1905

Web Sites

Har'El, Zvi. *Zvi Har'El's Jules Verne Collection*. 12 Sept. 2003. Last accessed 13 Dec. 2003. http://jv.gilead.org.il/.
Extensive site. Includes biographical information.

"Jules Verne." *CORAL (Caribbean Online Resource and Archive)*. 2002. Last accessed 22 Dec. 2003. http://www.caribbeanedu.com/coral/refcen/Biography/readbio.asp?id=247.
Biographical sketch.

"Jules Verne Bibliography." *Fantastic Fiction*. 2003. Last accessed 13 Dec. 2003. http://www.fantasticfiction.co.uk/authors/Jules_Verne.htm.
Lists Verne's major works.

Liukkonen, Petri. "Jules Verne." *Author's Calendar*. Ed. Ari Pesonen. 2000. Last accessed 13 Dec. 2003. http://www.kirjasto.sci.fi/verne.htm.
Biographical sketch and discussion of Verne's major works.

Project Gutenberg. 25 Dec. 2003. Last accessed 27 Dec. 2003. http://www.gutenberg.net/index.shtml.
Includes uncopyrighted online texts for several of Verne's works, including *20,000 Leagues Under the Sea* (use the "Find an Ebook" link to find texts by Verne).

Biographies and Criticism

Carter, Betty. "Verne, Jules." Silvey, *Children's Books and Their Creators*. 662–63.

Gonsior, Marian. "Jules Verne." *Authors and Artists for Young Adults* 16: 155–70.
Biographical sketch with portrait, discussion of major works.

"Jules Verne." *Children's Literature Review* 88: 108–89.
Biographical sketch, discussion of literary career, excerpts from reviews and commentary.

JUDITH VIORST, 1931–

Web Sites

"Alexander and the Terrible, Horrible, No Good, Very Bad Day." *Kennedy Center*. Last accessed 27 Dec. 2003. http://www.kennedy-center.org/programs/family/alexander/intro.html.
Web site for stage adaption of Viorst's book. Includes a biographical sketch on Viorst.

"Judith Viorst." *Academy of American Poets*. 2003. Last accessed 27 Dec. 2003. http://www.poets.org/poets/poets.cfm?prmID=62&CFID=2033175&CFTOKEN=42891650.
Biographical sketch. Includes links to related sites.

Witter, Dottie. "An Evening with Judith Viorst." *Friends of the OSU Library*. 13 June 2003. Last accessed 27 Dec. 2003. http://www.library.okstate.edu/friends/cobb/viorst.htm.
Written account of a 1997 presentation Viorst made at Oklahoma State University.

Biographies and Criticism

Cleghorn, Andrea. "Viorst, Judith." Silvey, *The Essential Guide to Children's Books and Their Creators*. 458–59.
Biographical sketch.

Jones, J. Sydney. "Viorst, Judith." *Something About the Author* 123: 171–79.
Biographical sketch with portrait, discussion of major works.

"Judith Viorst." *Children's Literature Review* 90: 150–65.
Biographical sketch, discussion of literary career, excerpts from reviews and commentary.

Street, Douglas. "Judith Viorst." Estes, *American Writers for Children Since 1960: Fiction* (*Dictionary of Literary Biography* 52): 368–73.
Discussion of literary career and influence.

CYNTHIA VOIGT, 1942–

Web Sites

Albritton, Tom. "Teaching, Learning, and Archetypes: Images of Instruction in Cynthia Voigt's *Dicey's Song*." *ALAN Review* 21: 3 (Spring 1994). Last accessed 13 Dec. 2003. http://scholar.lib.vt.edu/ejournals/ALAN/spring94/Albritton.html.
Critical essay.

"Cynthia Voigt." *Fantastic Fiction*. 2003. Last accessed 13 Dec. 2003. http://www.fantasticfiction.co.uk/authors/Cynthia_Voigt.htm.
Lists Voigt's major works.

Kerby, Mona. "Cynthia Voigt." *Mona Kerby's The Author's Corner*. Apr. 2003. Last accessed 13 Dec. 2003. http://www.carr.lib.md.us/mae/voigt/voigt.htm.
Brief biographical sketch, lists of awards Voigt has won, links to other online resources.

"Voigt, Cynthia." *Educational Paperback Association*. Last accessed 13 Dec. 2003. http://www.edupaperback.org/showauth.cfm?authid=109.
Biographical sketch with selected list of major works.

Biographies and Criticism

"Cynthia Voigt." *Children's Literature Review* 48: 148–86.
Biographical sketch, discussion of literary career, excerpts from reviews and commentary.

Gillis, Mary. "Voigt, Cynthia." *Something About the Author* 116. 214–19.
   Biographical sketch with portrait, discussion of major works.

Goldsmith, Francisca. "Voigt, Cynthia." Cullinan and Person, *The Continuum Encyclopedia of Children's Literature*. 801–2.
   Biographical sketch.

ROSEMARY WELLS, 1943–

Web Sites

Silvey, Anita. "Rosemary Wells Interviewed by Anita Silvey." *The Horn Book.*
   Last accessed 13 Dec. 2003. http://www.hbook.com/exhibit/wellsradio
   .html.
   Audio file and transcript of interview with Wells.

The World of Rosemary Wells. Last accessed 13 Dec. 2003. http://www
   .rosemarywells.com/.
   Author web site. Includes biographical information.

Biographies and Criticism

Goldsmith, Francisca. "Wells, Rosemary." Cullinan and Person, *The Continuum Encyclopedia of Children's Literature*. 810–12.
   Biographical sketch.

"Rosemary Wells." *Children's Literature Review* 69: 149–83.
   Biographical sketch, discussion of literary career, excerpts from reviews
and commentary.

Senick, Gerard J. "Wells, Rosemary." *Something About the Author* 114: 224–32.
   Biographical sketch with portrait, discussion of major works.

E. B. WHITE, 1899–1985

Web Sites

"E. B. White." *HarperChildrens.com.* Last accessed 27 Dec. 2003. http://
   www.harperchildrens.com/authorintro/index.asp?authorid=10499.
   Publisher web site. Includes biographical sketch, letter from E. B. White.

"E. B. White Collection." *Carl A. Kroch Library (Cornell University).* 4 Jan. 2002.
   Last accessed 13 Dec. 2003. http://rmc.library.cornell.edu/collections/
   subjects/ebwhite.html.
   Description of E. B. White archival collection at Cornell. Includes a biographical sketch.

Liukkonen, Petri. "E. B. White." *Author's Calendar.* Ed. Ari Pesonen. 2000. Last
   accessed 13 Dec. 2003. http://www.kirjasto.sci.fi/ebwhite.htm.
   Biographical sketch and discussion of White's major works.

"White, E. B." *Educational Paperback Association.* Last accessed 13 Dec. 2003. http://www.edupaperback.org/showauth.cfm?authid=77.
Biographical sketch with selected list of major works.

Biographies and Criticism

Agosta, Lucien L. *E. B. White: The Children's Books.* New York: Twayne Publishers, 1995.
Critical commentary on White's children's books.

"E(lywn) B(rooks) White." *Children's Literature Review* 21: 191–218.
Biographical sketch, discussion of literary career, excerpts from reviews and commentary.

Neumeyer, Peter F. "E. B. White." Cech, *American Writers for Children, 1900–1960* (*Dictionary of Literary Biography* 22): 333–50.
Discussion of literary career and influence.

———. "White, E. B." Silvey, *The Essential Guide to Children's Books and Their Creators.* 466–68.
Biographical sketch.

"White, E(lywn) B(rooks)." *Something About the Author* 100: 248–53.
Biographical sketch with portrait, discussion of major works.

Bibliographies

"White, E. B." Hendrickson, *Children's Literature: A Guide to the Criticism.* 283–86.
Lists books and articles about White and his works.

"White, E(lwin) B(rooks)." Lynn, *Fantasy Literature for Children and Young Adults.* 904–7.
Lists books and articles about White and his works.

T. H. WHITE, 1906–1964

Web Sites

"The Bestiary: A Book of Beasts." Ed. T. H. White. UW *Madison Libraries.* Last accessed 13 Dec. 2003. http://libtext.library.wisc.edu/cgi-bin/Bestiary/Bestiary-idx?type=header&issueid=Bestiary.Bestiary.
Online version of White's book.

Moulder, Jason W., and Marcus Schaefer. *"England Have My Bones": For the Readers of the Works of T. H. White.* 10 June 2003. Last accessed 13 Dec. 2003. http://www2.netdoor.com/~moulder/thwhite/.
Extensive site on White and his works.

"T. H. White—Life Stories, Books, and Links." *Today in Literature*. 2003. Last accessed 13 Dec. 2003. http://www.todayinliterature.com/biography/ t.h.white.asp.
Brief biographical sketch, links to related online resources.

Biographies and Criticism

Deifendeifer, Anne E. "White T. H." Silvey, *The Essential Guide to Children's Books and Their Creators*. 468–69.
Biographical sketch.

Keenan, Hugh T. "T. H. White." Hettinga and Schmidt, *British Children's Writers, 1914–1960 (Dictionary of Literary Biography* 160): 307–14.
Discussion of literary career and influence.

"White, T(erence) H(anbury)." *Something About the Author* 12: 229–38.
Biographical sketch with portrait, discussion of major works.

Bibliographies

Lynn, Ruth Nadelman. "White, T(erence) H(anbury)." *Fantasy Literature for Children and Young Adults*. 908–9.
Lists White's major works.

LAURA INGALLS WILDER, 1867–1957

Web Sites

"Laura Ingalls Wilder." *Deadwood Magazine*. Mar.-Apr. 1996. Last accessed 13 Dec. 2003. http://rapidweb.com/deadwoodmag/Laura.htm.
Biographical sketch.

Laura Ingalls Wilder: Frontier Girl. Last accessed 13 Dec. 2003. http:// webpages.marshall.edu/~irby1/laura.htmlx.
Extensive site. Includes biographical information.

Laura Ingalls Wilder Memorial Society, Inc. 2002. Last accessed 13 Dec. 2003. http://www.liwms.com/.
Includes biographical information.

Biographies and Criticism

Hunt, Sarah, and Peter Hunt. "Wilder, Laura Ingalls." Cullinan and Person, *The Continuum Encyclopedia of Children's Literature*. 818–19.
Biographical sketch.

Jones, J. Sydney. "Laura Ingalls Wilder." *Authors and Artists for Young Adults* 26: 195–205.
Biographical sketch with portrait, discussion of major works.

Piehl, Kathy. "Laura Ingalls Wilder." Cech, *American Writers for Children, 1900–1960 (Dictionary of Literary Biography* 22): 351–66.
Discussion of literary career and influence.

Romines, Ann. *Constructing the Little House: Gender, Culture, and Laura Ingalls Wilder*. Amherst: University of Massachusetts Press, 1997.
Book-length study of Wilder's *Little House* books.

"Wilder, Laura Ingalls." *Children's Literature Review* 2: 202–7.
Biographical sketch, discussion of literary career, excerpts from reviews and commentary.

Bibliographies

"Laura Ingalls Wilder." Rahn, *Children's Literature: An Annotated Bibliography of the History and Criticism*. 386–90.
Lists books and articles about Wilder and her works.

"Wilder, Laura Ingalls." Hendrickson, *Children's Literature: A Guide to the Criticism*. 287–91.
Lists books and articles about Wilder and her works.

ASHLEY WOLFF, 1956–

Web Sites

"Ashley Wolff." *Penguin Group (USA)*. 2000. Last accessed 13 Dec. 2003. http://www.penguinputnam.com/Author/AuthorFrame/?0000028095.
Publisher web site. Includes portrait, biographical sketch.

Biographies and Criticism

Cerra, Kathie Krieger. "Wolff, (Jenifer) Ashley." Cullinan and Person, *The Continuum Encyclopedia of Children's Literature*. 826.
Biographical sketch.

"Wolff, (Jenifer) Ashley." *Something About the Author* 81: 214–17.
Biographical sketch with portrait, discussion of major works.

DIANA WYNNE JONES, 1934–

Web Sites

"Diana Wynne Jones Bibliography." *Fantastic Fiction*. 2003. Last accessed 5 Dec. 2003. http://www.fantasticfiction.co.uk/authors/Diana_Wynne_Jones.htm.
Lists Wynne Jones's major works.

Kaplan, Deborah. *The Diana Wynne Jones Homepage*. 8 Aug. 2003. Last accessed 5 Dec. 2003. http://suberic.net/dwj/.
Includes biographical resources, information about Wynne Jones's books.

MacArdle, Meredith, and Helen Scott. *The Official Diana Wynne Jones Website.* 13 Nov. 2003. Last accessed 5 Dec. 2003. http://www.leemac.freeserve .co.uk/.
Includes material by Wynne Jones.

"The Many Worlds of Diana Wynne Jones." *HarperCollins Publishers.* Last accessed 5 Dec. 2003. http://www.dianawynnejones.com.
Publisher web site. Includes biographical information.

Biographies and Criticism

"Diana Wynne Jones." *Children's Literature Review* 23: 177–98.
Biographical sketch, discussion of literary career, excerpts from reviews and commentary.

Jones, J. Sydney. "Jones, Diana Wynne." *Something About the Author* 108: 123–29.
Biographical sketch with portrait, discussion of major works.

Kantar, Andrew. "Wynne Jones, Diana." Cullinan and Person, *The Continuum Encyclopedia of Children's Literature.* 831–32.
Biographical sketch.

White, Donna R. "Diana Wynne Jones." Hunt, *British Children's Writers Since 1960 (Dictionary of Literary Biography* 161): 225–32.
Discussion of literary career and influence.

LAURENCE YEP, 1948–

Web Sites

Gendell, Adrienne, and Maggie Hanley, with Kay E. Vandergrift. "Learning about Laurence Yep." *Vandergrift's Children's Literature Page.* 20 Nov. 1996. Last accessed 13 Dec. 2003. http://scils.rutgers.edu/~kvander/yep.html.
Biographical sketch, list of selected works.

"Laurence Yep." *Penguin Group (USA).* 2000. Last accessed 13 Dec. 2003. http://www.penguinputnam.com/Author/AuthorFrame?0000028405.
Biographical sketch from publisher web site.

"Laurence Yep Bibliography." *Fantastic Fiction.* 2003. Last accessed 13 Dec. 2003. http://www.fantasticfiction.co.uk/authors/Laurence_Yep.htm.
Lists Yep's major works.

Biographies and Criticism

Jones, J. Sydney. "Yep, Laurence." *Something About the Author* 123: 192–97.
Biographical sketch with portrait, discussion of major works.

"Laurence Michael Yep." *Children's Literature Review* 54: 175–204.
Biographical sketch, discussion of literary career, excerpts from reviews and commentary.

Stines, Joe. "Laurence Yep." Estes, *American Writers for Children Since 1960: Fiction* (*Dictionary of Literary Biography* 52): 392–98.
Discussion of literary career and influence.

Wilson, Nance S. "Yep, Laurence." Cullinan and Person, *The Continuum Encyclopedia of Children's Literature*. 836–37.
Biographical sketch.

JANE YOLEN, 1939–

Web Sites

The Book on Jane Yolen. 23 Nov. 2003. Last accessed 13 Dec. 2003. http://www.janeyolen.com/.
Author web site. Includes biographical information.

Horak, Lisa. "After 25 years, Yolen still provides children with 'quiet friends.'" *BookPage*. Last accessed 13 Dec. 2003. http://www.bookpage.com/ 9901bp/jane_yolen.html.
Portrait; interview with Yolen.

"Jane Yolen." *KidSpace @ The Internet Public Library*. 1995. Last accessed 13 Dec. 2003. http://ipl.sils.umich.edu/div/kidspace/askauthor/Yolen.html.
Biographical sketch.

"Jane Yolen." *Penguin Group (USA)*. 2000. Last accessed 13 Dec. 2003. http://www.penguinputnam.com/Author/AuthorFrame?0000028422.
Biographical sketch from publisher web site.

"Jane Yolen Bibliography." *Fantastic Fiction*. 2003. Last accessed 13 Dec. 2003. http://www.fantasticfiction.co.uk/authors/Jane_Yolen.htm.
Lists Yolen's major works.

Perry, Evelyn. "Poetry and Archaeology: Narration in Contemporary Retellings of Folk and Fairy Tales for Young Adults: Jane Yolen's *Briar Rose*." *The Looking Glass* 7: 2 (2 Apr. 2003). http://www.the-looking-glass.net/rabbit/v7i2/curious.html.
Critical essay.

Biographies and Criticism

"Autobiography Feature: Jane Yolen." *Something About the Author* 111: 203–25.
Autobiographical sketch.

"Jane Yolen." *Children's Literature Review* 44: 167–211.
Biographical sketch, discussion of literary career, excerpts from reviews and commentary.

Kreuger, William E. "Jane Yolen." Estes, *American Writers for Children Since 1960: Fiction* (*Dictionary of Literary Biography* 52): 398–405.
Discussion of literary career and influence.

Senick, Gerard J. "Yolen, Jane (Hyatt)." *Something About the Author* 112: 207–21.
Biographical sketch with portrait, discussion of major works.

Sieruta, Peter D. "Yolen, Jane." Silvey, *The Essential Guide to Children's Books and Their Creators*. 484–85.
Biographical sketch.

Bibliographies

Lynn, Ruth Nadelman. "Yolen (Stemple), Jane H(yatt)." *Fantasy Literature for Children and Young Adults*. 919–20.
Lists books and articles about Yolen and her works.

PAUL ZINDEL, 1936–2003

Web Sites

"Paul Zindel Bibliography." *Fantastic Fiction*. 2003. Last accessed 13 Dec. 2003.
http://www.fantasticfiction.co.uk/authors/Paul_Zindel.htm.
Lists Zindel's major works.

"Zindel, Paul." *Educational Paperback Association*. Last accessed 13 Dec. 2003.
http://www.edupaperback.org/showauth.cfm?authid=86.
Biographical sketch with list of major works.

Zindel, Paul. "Journey to Meet the Pigman." *ALAN Review* 22: 1 (Fall 1994).
http://scholar.lib.vt.edu/ejournals/ALAN/fall94/Zindel.html.
Autobiographical piece by Zindel on writing *The Pigman*.

Biographies and Criticism

Hipple, Theodore W. "Paul Zindel." Estes, *American Writers for Children Since 1960: Fiction* (*Dictionary of Literary Biography* 52): 405–10.
Discussion of literary career and influence.

"Paul Zindel." *Children's Literature Review* 85: 150–89.
Biographical sketch, discussion of literary career, excerpts from reviews and commentary.

Senick, Gerard J. "Paul Zindel." *Authors and Artists for Young Adults* 37: 195–206.
Biographical sketch with portrait, discussion of major works.

Tchana, Katrin. "Zindel, Paul." Silvey, *The Essential Guide to Children's Books and Their Creators*. 495–96.
Biographical sketch.

Bibliographies

"Zindel, Paul." Hendrickson, *Children's Literature: A Guide to the Criticism*. 296–98.
Lists books and articles about Zindel and his works.

CHARLOTTE ZOLOTOW, 1915–

Web Sites

"Author Tracker: Charlotte Zolotow." *HarperCollins.* Last accessed 27 Dec. 2003.
http://www.harpercollins.com/catalog/author_xml.asp?AuthorId=12952.
Biographical sketch from publisher web site.

"Charlotte Zolotow." *KidSpace @ The Internet Public Library.* Last accessed 13
Dec. 2003. http://www.ipl.org/div/kidspace/askauthor/Zolotow.html.
Biographical sketch; interview with Zolotow.

"Charlotte Zolotow." *Wisconsin Authors and Illustrators.* Last accessed 13 Dec.
2003. http://www.soemadison.wisc.edu/ccbc/wisauth/zolotow/main.htm.
Biographical sketch and list of her major works.

The Charlotte Zolotow Web Site. 22 Mar. 2003. Last accessed 13 Dec. 2003.
http://www.charlottezolotow.com/index.htm.
Author web site. Includes biographical information.

Biographies and Criticism

"Charlotte Zolotow." *Children's Literature Review* 77: 155–78.
Biographical sketch, discussion of literary career, excerpts from reviews
and commentary.

Francis, Elizabeth. "Charlotte Zolotow." Estes, *American Writers for Children
Since 1960: Fiction* (*Dictionary of Literary Biography* 52): 411–18.
Discussion of literary career and influence.

Sutherland, Zena. "Zolotow, Charlotte." Silvey, *The Essential Guide to Children's
Books and Their Creators.* 496–97.
Biographical sketch.

"Zolotow, Charlotte (Gertrude)." *Something About the Author* 138: 228–36.
Biographical sketch with portrait, discussion of major works.

Index of Authors

Ada, Alma Flor, 11

Adams, Richard, 12

Adler, David, 13

Aiken, Joan, 13

Alcott, Louisa May, 14

Aldrich, Thomas Bailey, 15

Alexander, Lloyd, 16

Alger, Horatio, Jr., 17

Aliki, 18

Andersen, Hans Christian, 19

Armstrong, William H., 20

Austen, Jane, 20

Avi, 21

Awdry, Wilbert Vere, 22

Babbitt, Natalie, 23

Bagnold, Enid, 24

Ballantyne, R. M., 24

Barrie, J. M., 25

Baum, L. Frank, 26

Bawden, Nina, 27

Bellairs, John, 28

Bemelmans, Ludwig, 28

Berenstain, Jan, 29

Berenstain, Stan, 29

Block, Francesca Lia, 30

Blume, Judy, 31

Blyton, Enid, 32

Bond, Michael, 33

Brandenburg, Aliki. *See* Aliki

Bridgers, Sue Ellen, 33

Briggs, Raymond, 34

Brooks, Gwendolyn, 34

Brown, Marc, 36

Brown, Margaret Wise, 36

Bruchac, Joseph, 37

Bunting, Eve, 38

Burnett, Frances Hodgson, 38

Burton, Virginia Lee, 39

Byars, Betsy, 40

Cabot, Meg, 41

Carle, Eric, 41

Carroll, Lewis. *See* Dodgson, Charles
    Lutwidge

Child, Lydia Maria, 42

Christopher, John, 43

Ciardi, John, 43

Cisneros, Sandra, 44

Cleary, Beverly, 45

Clemens, Samuel Langhorne (Mark
    Twain), 46

Clifton, Lucille, 47

Coatsworth, Elizabeth, 47

Collodi, Carlo (Carlo Lorenzini), 48

Cooney, Barbara, 49

Cooney, Caroline, 50
Cooper, Susan, 50
Cormier, Robert, 51
Creech, Sharon, 52
Crutcher, Chris, 53
Cushman, Karen, 53

Dahl, Roald, 54
Danziger, Paula, 55
de Angeli, Marguerite, 56
de Brunhoff, Jean, 56
de Brunhoff, Laurent, 56
Defoe, Daniel, 57
dePaola, Tomie, 58
Dickens, Charles, 58
Dodgson, Charles Lutwidge (Lewis
    Carroll), 59
Doyle, Arthur Conan, 61
du Bois, William Pène, 62
Duncan, Lois, 62

Engdahl, Sylvia, 63
Erdrich, Louise, 64

Farley, Walter, 65
Fitzhugh, Louise, 65
Fleischman, Sid, 66
Fox, Paula, 67
Frank, Anne, 67
Fritz, Jean, 68

Gág, Wanda, 68
Gaiman, Neil, 69
Geisel, Theodor Seuss (Dr. Seuss), 70
George, Jean Craighead, 71
Gipson, Fred, 72
Gorey, Edward, 72
Grahame, Kenneth, 73
Greenaway, Kate, 74
Greenfield, Eloise, 74

Grimes, Nikki, 75
Grimm, Jacob Ludwig Karl, 76
Grimm, Wilhelm Karl, 76
Gruelle, Johnny, 77

Hamilton, Virginia, 77
Handler, Daniel (Lemony Snicket), 78
Harris, Joel Chandler (Uncle Remus),
    78
Henkes, Kevin, 79
Hinton, S. E., 80
Hoban, Lillian, 81
Hoban, Russell, 81
Hughes, Ted, 82

Jacques, Brian, 83
Jarrell, Randall, 83
Johnson, Crockett, 84
Joyce, William, 84

Keats, Ezra Jack, 85
Kerr, M. E., 86
Kipling, Rudyard, 87
Konigsburg, E. L., 88

Lamb, Charles, 88
Lamb, Mary Ann, 88
Lang, Andrew, 89
Lawson, Robert, 90
Lear, Edward, 91
Le Guin, Ursula K., 92
L'Engle, Madeleine, 93
Lenski, Lois, 94
Lester, Julius, 94
Levine, Gail, 95
Lewis, C. S., 95
Lindgren, Astrid, 96
Lobel, Arnold, 97
Lofting, Hugh, 98
London, Jack, 98

Lorenzini, Carlo. *See* Collodi,
    Carlo
Lowry, Lois, 99

Macaulay, David, 100
MacDonald, George, 101
McCaffrey, Anne, 102
McCloskey, Robert, 103
McKinley, Robin, 103
Milne, A. A., 104
Minarik, Else Holmelund, 105
Montgomery, L. M., 105
Mora, Pat, 106
Myers, Walter Dean, 107

Nash, F. Ogden, 108
Nesbit, Edith, 108
Norton, Andre, 109
Norton, Mary, 109

O'Brien, Robert C., 111
O'Dell, Scott, 112

Paterson, Katherine, 112
Paton Walsh, Jill (Gillian), 114
Peck, Richard, 114
Peck, Robert Newton, 115
Pinkwater, Daniel, 115
Poe, Edgar Allan, 116
Potter, Beatrix, 117
Pullman, Philip, 118

Ransome, Arthur, 119
Raschka, Chris, 120
Raskin, Ellen, 120
Rawlings, Marjorie Kinnan, 121
Rey, H. A., 121
Rey, Margret, 121
Rossetti, Christina Georgina, 122
Rowling, J. K., 123

Saint-Exupéry, Antoine de, 124
Scarry, Richard, 124
Scieszka, Jon, 125
Sendak, Maurice, 125
Seredy, Kate, 126
Seuss, Dr. *See* Geisel, Theodor Seuss
Sewell, Anna, 127
Silverstein, Shel, 128
Singer, Isaac Bashevis, 128
Sleator, William, 129
Snicket, Lemony. *See* Handler,
    Daniel
Snyder, Zilpha Keatley, 130
Soto, Gary, 130
Speare, Elizabeth George, 131
Spinelli, Jerry, 132
Spyri, Johanna, 132
Steig, William, 133
Stevenson, Robert Louis, 133
Stine, R. L., 134
Stratemeyer, Edward L., 135

Taylor, Mildred D., 136
Thurber, James, 137
Tolkien, J.R.R., 137
Townsend, Sue, 138
Travers, P. L., 139
Twain, Mark. *See* Clemens, Samuel
    Langhorne

Uncle Remus. *See* Harris, Joel
    Chandler

Van Allsburg, Chris, 140
Verne, Jules, 141
Viorst, Judith, 142
Voigt, Cynthia, 142

Wells, Rosemary, 143
White, E. B., 143

White, T. H., 144

Wilder, Laura Ingalls, 145

Wolff, Ashley, 146

Wortis, Avi. *See* Avi

Wynne Jones, Diana, 146

Yep, Laurence, 147

Yolen, Jane, 148

Zindel, Paul, 149

Zolotow, Charlotte, 150

About the Author

JEN STEVENS received her MLIS from the University of Texas, Austin. She joined the staff of Washington State University Libraries, Pullman, where she began as a Humanities Reference Librarian. Since, she has been Interim Head of the George B. Brain Education Library at Washington State University. Jen is presently the Humanities Reference/Liaison Librarian at George Mason University in Fairfax, Virginia.